# UNDERSTANDING FUNDAMENTALISM

# UNDERSTANDING FUNDAMENTALISM

## CHRISTIAN, ISLAMIC, AND JEWISH MOVEMENTS

Richard T. Antoun

**ALTAMIRA**
PRESS

A Division of Rowman & Littlefield Publishers, Inc.
Walnut Creek • Lanham • New York • Oxford

PRESS

A Division of Rowman & Littlefield Publishers, Inc.
1630 North Main Street, #367
Walnut Creek, CA 94596
www.altamirapress.com

Rowman & Littlefield Publishers, Inc.
4720 Boston Way
Lanham, MD 20706

12 Hid's Copse Road
Cumnor Hill, Oxford OX2 9JJ, England

British Library Cataloguing in Publication Information Available

**Library of Congress Cataloging-in-Publication Data**

Antoun, Richard T.
  Understanding fundamentalism : Christian, Islamic, and Jewish movements / Richard T. Antoun.
    p. cm.
  Includes bibliographical references and index.
  ISBN 0-7591-0005-5 (alk. paper)—ISBN 0-7591-0006-3 (pbk. : alk. paper)
    1. Religious fundamentalism. I. Title.

BL238 .A58 2001
200'.9'04—dc21

                                                    2001022049

Printed in the United States of America

♾™ The paper used in this publication meets the minimum requirements of American
National Standard for Information Sciences—Permanence of Paper for Printed Library
Materials, ANSI/NISO Z39.48-1992.

# Contents

# Preface

In evaluating any book it is important for the reader to know who wrote it and how it came to be. I am a professional social anthropologist who has been conducting research in the Middle East, on and off, for almost four decades, mainly in Jordan, to a lesser degree in Iran, and peripherally in Egypt and Lebanon. I am also an American professor who came of age in the comfortable and relatively secure post–World War II period, part of a nation that subsequently waged one "cold" and three "hot" wars; a nation that moved, ever more rapidly and cumulatively, from a radio to a television to an audiotape/VCR to a computer/cell phone/Internet civilization. This book reflects these facts.

What is an anthropological perspective? An anthropological perspective takes seriously what people say and do and tries to understand their sayings and doings in their own terms without judging their "truth" or "falsity." This attitude does not imply that one has to surrender one's own beliefs, but it does imply that one has to appreciate other perspectives. The anthropologist aims for empathy rather than sympathy.

The social anthropologist focuses on what (all) the people say and do and not just on what the specialists (who are often elites) say and do. In the case at hand this implies that popular religion is as much a subject of our study as specialist religion. This book is not just about religion as interpreted by ministers, priests, rabbis, and 'ulema (Muslim religious scholars/leaders); it is also about religion as believed and practiced by laypersons. After recording what people say and do the social anthropologist seeks to explain or interpret what she or he has observed or recorded in some framework (e.g., universalistic, relativistic, evolutionist). The framework of interpretation chosen here is comparative and the central explanatory concept is fundamentalism.

Rather than questionnaires, surveys, or statistical analysis (although these techniques are also employed), participant observation is the key technique of the social anthropological perspective. That is, the anthropologist lives among the people being studied on a day-to-day basis, and through systematic observation and interaction over an extended period (initially for at least a year) records their way of life. In this case I have done so intensively only for Muslims in Jordan and Iran. For Christians and Jews I have drawn on my own observations as a member of American society over a lifetime as well as on scholarly and journalistic accounts of others who have written based on participant observation.

The subject of this book, fundamentalism, necessarily requires an orientation toward religion. For the social anthropologist, religion is based on genuine experience and not superstition (as for instance was the case for Sigmund Freud).[1] Anthropologists differ on the content of that experience: affective collective experience; the structure of interpersonal relations in the family; the cognitive and expressive problems of suffering, evil, and bafflement; or dreams.[2] Anthropologists consider religion true for other than theological reasons. That is, religion is based on genuine human experience, whether cognitive, emotional, or instrumental, and in that sense authentic. In their professional work, anthropologists do not endorse or deny the theological claims of particular religions (although, of course, they have their own beliefs). This conclusion leads us to another, namely, that anthropologists take a phenomenal rather than a noumenal view of religion. This means that they recognize that they are viewing religious belief and practice as outsiders and therefore are always at several removes from any "true account" of religious experience.

Finally, an anthropological view of religion must consciously take stock of the "self" in any research as much as the "other" that is studied. In the new "critical anthropology" that has become part of the anthropologist's craft at the end of the century, he or she must recognize the impact of the researcher's background/biases on the description and analysis produced.

To take stock of the self in this study I must briefly discuss my own religious genealogy so readers can assess from their own perspectives the question of researcher bias or, to put it less elegantly but more succinctly, "where I'm coming from."

My paternal grandfather, an immigrant from Lebanon to the United States at the end of the nineteenth century, was "religiously unmusical," or one might also say ecumenical in his thinking.[3] When the local Catholic priest in the Massachusetts town where he lived came to ask him to become a member of the local parish, he told him that he would just as soon worship in the mosque as the church! My maternal grandfather, a Brazilian journalist whom I never met, on the other hand, was a pacifist, staunch agnostic, and highly anticlerical (according to my mother), perhaps because of the sectarian troubles that had overwhelmed Lebanon in the previous century. He translated the lectures of Robert Ingersoll, a well-known American atheist, in his newspaper, a newspaper he published in Sao Paulo until 1936. He also published in it a cartoon of a fat priest driving away beggars from the door of the church at the same time that he retrieved the money from the charity box on the same door and took it into the church.

My paternal grandmother reflected another side of my religious background. She was a follower of the Eastern Catholic rite, which had not yet built a church in central Massachusetts. The local Roman Catholic priest had come and asked her to become a member of his parish church in the 1930s. Regretfully, she declined, saying that her own religious community was building its own (Melkite or Eastern Catholic) church, which it subsequently did. She often urged me to accompany her to Sunday worship services, which were held in a Semitic language (not Arabic) that neither my grandmother nor I could understand. Of course, I was not eager to do this, and seldom went with her. But in her later years I drove my grandmother to church and picked her up at the end of the service. On one of these occasions at a time when I had returned to my hometown tired and beset with a mild case of the flu on a midterm break from graduate school, I picked my grandmother up from church. As she got in the car she handed me a small urn of what I presumed to be holy water. She told me to drink it, and I would feel better. I refused. She pressed it on me. My Protestant sensitivities took hold (I went to a Methodist Sunday school), and I refused again. Suddenly, she took the urn and spilled it over my face! My grandmother was endowed with a spontaneous religious nature. She was a true believer in the church and the power of the holy to work its wonders in this world.

My mother and father were married in a civil marriage ceremony in Brazil and then were married in the Methodist church after coming to the United States. As a result, I suppose, and because it was close by, my sisters and I were sent to Methodist Sunday school. I can remember attending only basketball games and other strictly secular activities as part of my Sunday school upbringing. I remember getting no religious education whatsoever there, and that might account in part for my own interest in religion when I began teaching in the university. Perhaps I felt somehow ignorant or cheated about a subject I needed to know more about.

In the following years I attended Quaker meetings, the Lutheran church, and the Unitarian church, all without becoming a member. My exposure to the Unitarian tradition was far more than my experience with the others, particularly after my parents became members of one local Unitarian church and my brother-in-law became the minister of another in the local area. More recently I have been introduced to Judaism, particularly the Reform tradition, through my wife in a small city in upstate New York.

Certainly my most profound immersion in a religious tradition occurred in 1959 when I took up residence for a year in a small Sunni Muslim village in Jordan to undertake Ph.D. dissertation research. In the course of my stay there I became friends with the village preacher, entered the mosque every Friday, listened to his sermon, read the Quran with him on a weekly basis, and fasted the month of Ramadan with other villagers out of respect for their traditions. Based on these sermons I later wrote a book on how the tradition of Islam was presented in a peasant village environment.[4] In the first fifteen years of my research in the village, I studiously avoided debating religious, particularly theological, matters. After a number of visits there in the 1960s and 1970s, I regarded my presence in the village as unproblematic, until 1986 when, for the first time, persistent attempts were made, particularly by young men, to argue with me about religious matters and to convert me to Islam. No one had ever done so before.[5] This change in the religious ethos of the village forced me to begin reconsidering the question of religious change and religious belief and their relationship to social change in general.

I had been teaching an undergraduate course in comparative religion and symbolism for seventeen years, largely out of curiosity: a desire to learn more about a subject (religion) about which I knew a great deal with respect to a tradition that was not my own (Islam) but very little about my own (Christian) and other religious traditions.

In the late 1980s I began teaching a course on religious fundamentalism, considering the three monotheistic traditions, Islam, Christianity, and Judaism. This teaching was triggered in part by my latest fieldwork experience, but also by the resurgence of Christian fundamentalism in the United States, Jewish fundamentalism in Israel, and Muslim fundamentalism in Iran and Egypt, the latter being places where I had conducted research or lived. In this course I was concerned not only with considering the theoretical and contextual aspects of the phenomenon, but also its experiential and humanistic aspects. As much as possible, I chose books, films, and visiting lecturers that allowed the members of the different religious traditions to speak for themselves—and not just be spoken for. I have attempted to follow that policy in this book as well.

A few caveats are in order to alert the reader about what this book does *not* claim or do. It is neither a defense nor a critique of fundamentalism as an ideology or way of life. It is not a historical study. It does not aim at explaining how fundamentalist movements develop in particular places at particular times. I am not a historian, although I do have an appreciation of historical studies.

The aim of this book is to identify themes that cut across the three monotheistic traditions to bring out the commonalities in thought and action, belief and practice. The study is by intent comparative, and being so, cannot trace in a detailed manner the development of particular movements. No doubt, a discussion of Hindu, Sikh, or Buddhist fundamentalism would be valuable and make this study more widely cross-cultural, but such a study is beyond my expertise.[6]

Confining the study to the monotheistic religions has the advantage of being able to compare in a more intensive and systematic way familiar themes that appear in different forms in the three monotheistic traditions. The religious traditions of Islam, Christianity, and Judaism, after all, are intimately related not only historically but also theologically. Muslims recognize the Hebrew prophets and even include Jesus as one of them! Moreover, all three religions accept Abraham as a significant seminal figure in their religious tradition and recognize that they share a common legacy.

This book, then, is a restricted cross-cultural comparison of the phenomenon of fundamentalism, defined in this book as an orientation to the world, a particular worldview and ethos, and as a movement of protest and outrage against the rapid change that has overtaken the people of an increasingly global civilization at the end of the twentieth century. The study selects a number of (but not all) prominent themes that define the belief and practice of fundamentalism.[7] Whereas most studies of fundamentalism focus on scripturalism (the literal belief in an inerrant sacred scripture), in this study scripturalism assumes its position as only one of a number of important themes that, altogether, identify fundamentalists wherever they are: the search for purity in an impure world; "traditioning" (making the ancient immediately relevant to the contemporary situation); totalism (taking religion out of the worship center and into many other domains; e.g., the home, the school, the bank); activism (confronting establishments, political or religious, by protest, sometimes violent); the struggle of good and evil; and selective modernization and controlled acculturation.

Because the focus here is on diverse fundamentalist themes that appear and reappear in various fundamentalist movements, it should be clear that no single person designated as a fundamentalist possesses all attributes of belief and practice. In that sense, fundamentalism is an ideal type with living human beings only imperfectly fitting the description. On the human level, we are dealing with a continuum of people who are more or less "fundamentalist" according to the number of themes embraced. In an imperfect world this result should not be surprising.

I wish to thank my undergraduate students at the State University of New York at Binghamton who have attended my classes on religious fundamentalism over the last ten years and discussed, debated, and often challenged my views orally and in written papers, and thereby helped me to develop my ideas about the subject. I also wish to thank colleagues and friends for taking time out of busy schedules to read the manuscript in part or in whole and to offer helpful comments and criticisms. In particular I wish to thank Ricardo Laremont, Bruce Lawrence, David Miller, Dick Moench, James Preston, Spyros Spyrou, Helen Rivlin, and the anonymous reviewers appointed by Alta Mira Press. I also wish to thank Tony King and the Braudel Center for the invitation to present my ideas to the Seminar on Religion in the autumn of 1997. Finally, thanks are due to the sponsoring editor of Alta Mira Press, Erik Hanson, and its production editor, Dorothy Bradley, for shepherding the manuscript through the vicissitudes of editing and publication.

## Notes

1. See Sigmund Freud, *The Future of an Illusion*, ed. James Strachey, trans. W. D. Robson-Scott (London: Hogarth Press: Institute of Psycho-analysis, 1962), for this view.
2. See the articles by Emile Durkheim and Edward Tylor in William Lessa's and Evon Vogt's *Reader in Comparative Religion: An Anthropological Approach*, 4th ed. (New York: Harper and Row, 1979), and the articles by Clifford Geertz and Melford Spiro in Michael Banton's *Anthropological Approaches to the Study of Religion* (New York: F.A. Praeger, 1966), for examples of anthropological writing on religion.
3. The phrase "religiously unmusical" was coined by the well-known sociologist of religion Max Weber.
4. See Richard Antoun, *Muslim Preacher in the Modern World: A Jordanian Case Study in Comparative Perspective*, 1989.
5. Of course, my presence had always been problematic. As an American, an unmarried adult, and a man of Christian origin, particularly one who took such a strong interest in Islam (and had read the Quran without converting), I was "marked" as different. But before 1986 I did not recognize this status because

after all, villagers were hospitable and cooperative, and the mayor and preacher of the village facilitated my work and welcomed me, as I did them, on all occasions.

6. South Asians have certainly pursued a wide variety of orientations and strategies to cope with change in the modern world including fundamentalism. In fact, India's Bharatiya Janata Party is the largest movement of religious nationalism in the world. Its victory in the Indian elections of 1999 allowed it to form the governing coalition at the national level. Sikh fundamentalists have been active for many years as a movement fighting both secular nationalism and Hindu nationalism. The selective bibliography at the end of the book includes titles on fundamentalism in South and Southeast Asia for interested readers.

7. For instance, millennialism is an important theme of fundamentalist movements. It is not treated in this book. The struggle between good and evil is another important theme to which I have given some attention, but not nearly what it deserves. The same can be said for the theme of the search for authenticity.

# INTRODUCTION

At the turn of the twentieth century, Americans, Europeans, and residents of the Third World have become concerned to varying degrees with crises related to energy and environmental depletion, overpopulation, the impact of mass media, transnational migration and cultural and economic globalization, rapid computerization, crime, drugs, and family instability. Also viewed as a coequal threat, but not necessarily associated with them in any causal sense, is religious fundamentalism. Popular and journalistic views of religious fundamentalism focus in the Christian case on religious bigotry, scandalous beliefs (e.g., for self-styled enlightened Christians, the fundamentalist belief in Christ's imminent return on "clouds of glory"), opposition to science in general and to the doctrine of evolution in particular, puritanical sexual ethics, and xenophobia. In the Muslim case the focus is on the repression of women, including their veiling, seclusion, and confinement; harsh and often brutal punishments for violation of religious norms; fanaticism of beliefs; hostility to westerners; patriarchalism; and the tendency to resort to violence within the national community and to terrorism outside it. In the Jewish case, popular and journalistic views center on rigid thought patterns and doctrinaire beliefs, an archaic style of life, an ethos of violent retaliation for wrongs done, intolerance of differences within the religious tradition and hostility to those outside it, patriarchalism, and resistance to assimilation. All fundamentalists are generally viewed as doctrinaire followers of sacred scripture, dwellers

1

in and on the past, and naive simplifiers of complex world events involved in a struggle between good and evil.[1]

This book, on the other hand, regards religious fundamentalism as a much broader phenomenon, as an orientation to the modern world, both cognitive and emotional, that focuses on protest and change and on certain consuming themes: the quest for purity, the search for authenticity, totalism and activism, the necessity of certainty (scripturalism), selective modernization, and the centering of the mythic past in the present. *Totalism* is the religious orientation that views religion as relevant to all important domains of culture and society including politics, the family, the marketplace, education, and law. *Scripturalism* is the justification and reference of all important beliefs and acts to a sacred scripture held to be inerrant. *Selective modernization* is the process of selective and controlled acceptance of technological and social organizational innovations introduced by the modern world. Finally, centering of the mythic past in the present (*traditioning*) is the process of making scriptural accounts, events, and images relevant to present day-to-day activities. Each of these themes will be explored in the chapters that follow.

Fundamentalism is only one response to the "cultural disqualification of all traditions bearing a unified code of meaning in a world committed to rapid change and pluralization."[2] That is, fundamentalism is a response to the questioning of the great religious traditions—Islam, Christianity, Judaism, Buddhism, Hinduism—in the changing world. It is the one selected for study because at the end of one century and the beginning of another, fundamentalism is a transnational religious phenomenon that has entered many domains of culture and social organization with startling consequences for the individual, the intimate social group, and the nation-state.

Many academics and members of the three faiths designated by others as "fundamentalists" repudiate the usage of the term for themselves and, in so doing, the right of anyone else to so designate them. Many Jews and Muslims, in particular, deny the relevance of the term fundamentalist for themselves, arguing that historically the term originated with Protestants at the end of the nineteenth century. They hold that the term cannot be transferred to other religious traditions that are historically unrelated.[3] A historian of religion, Bruce Lawrence has termed this argument "exclusion by origin." He has pointed out that by the same argument, "one may not speak of nationalism in the Middle East since most Arabs and many Iranians reject the European experience as an authentic antecedent mediating their own entrance into the twentieth century as a nation-state."[4] However, as many scholars have attested, nationalism is an easily portable global transplant regardless of its origin.[5] The other argument that reserves the use of a term only to those who claim it for themselves is equally weak, because "by that logic, the only humanists are those who claim to be humanists; there are no teachers but those who teach in classrooms; and clowns only are found in circuses."[6]

This book will use the phrase *religious fundamentalism* as a cross-culturally applicable concept to a wide variety of religious traditions at a certain point in modern history. Fundamentalism does not refer so much to a set of dogmatic beliefs, to a creed, or to a literal adherence to a sacred text considered infallible. Rather, more broadly it refers to an orientation to the world, both cognitive and affective.[7] The affective, or emotional, orientation indicates outrage and protest against (and also fear of) change and against a certain ideological orientation, the orientation of modernism. Ideology refers here to "an action-oriented system of beliefs capable of explaining the world . . . justifying decision(s), identifying alternatives, and . . . creating the most all-embracing and intensive social solidarity possible."[8] In short, an ideology is an action-related system of ideas focused on this (and not the next) world. Whereas religions tend to support the status quo, ideologies tend to oppose it.[9] Fundamentalist movements are defined, ideologically, by their opposition to and reaction against the ideology that suits the permissive secular society, the ideology of modernism. Lawrence has characterized the ideology of modernism as one that values change over continuity, quantity over quality, and commercial efficiency (production and profit) over human sympathy for traditional values.[10] Modernism is an ideology for a society that prizes consumer-oriented capitalism, competition, specialization, and mobility while repudiating hierarchy. The ethos of fundamentalism, its affective orientation, is one of protest and outrage at the secularization of society; that is, at the process by which religion and its spirit has been steadily removed from public life—from schools, offices, workshops, universities, courts, and markets, and even from religious institutions themselves—churches, mosques, and synagogues.

The fundamentalist worldview, the repudiation of the cumulative changes instituted by the secularized society and their replacement by religious ethics and purified religious institutions, can be intuitively understood by the members of a global society who are constantly subject to change in their daily lives. But the fundamentalist ethos is not so easily understood and deserves elaboration.

## Change over Continuity

Let us consider the elevation of change over continuity in our lives. Since the breakup of the AT&T monopoly of long-distance telephone calling in the last decade of the twentieth century, middle-class Americans have been inundated by various telephone companies competing with one another for customers, with telephone subscriber scams being a part of the competition. The constant upgrading of computer hardware and software and the constant necessity for users of word processors to upgrade their machines, their programs, and their skills is a familiar part of the way of life of middle-class Americans. In the state university where I work, attrition of the professorial workforce caused by state budget cuts to higher education has resulted in an increasing number of graduate students teaching undergraduate courses. Students can no longer depend on being taught by a professor with an advanced degree. And the graduate students themselves have become a part of a burgeoning part-time workforce that is unstable and insecure because it lacks the normal perquisites of full-time jobs including health and pension benefits. Whereas job insecurity may be greater than at any time since the great depression, among large corporations job mobility has been a standard expectation since World War II. A best seller, The Organization Man, written by a sociologist shortly after World War II, described the lives of corporation families who constantly had to uproot and adjust to the new suburbs where they relocated.[11] So common a part of life in corporate America and Europe is this phenomenon that it has been termed *spiralism* by sociologists: one has to move spatially to climb hierarchically. My next-door neighbor, a thirty-year veteran engineer for a large corporation is, along with his wife and family, a lover of upper New York state where he works. Every few years this corporation has pressured him to move to another location to climb the ladder of the company hierarchy (i.e., to become a "spiralist"). He and his family wished to remain in upper New York state. The only way his company allowed him to accomplish that feat was by agreeing to work the night shift, (midnight to 8 A.M.) every third year. This was the price of continuity! Before the industrial revolution the overwhelming majority of the world's people literally worked where they lived, and they lived in one place! Although human beings in peasant societies traveled to regional markets, they worked daily within walking distance of their homes, enabling cultivators to go out to their fields and return by night-fall. The urban revolution did not usually disrupt the unity of home and work; it was quite common for urban dwellers in the Chinese, Indian, and Middle Eastern civilizations to live in the same neighborhood where they worked; often, they lived and worked in the same building, working on the first floor, living on the second.[12] The industrial revolution changed all that. The introduction of the factory required leaving one's home to go to work. During the last one hundred years, and particularly in the last twenty-five, the industrial revolution and the high-tech era have encouraged the rapid spread of transportation and communication networks, triggering mobility because of the proliferation of job opportunities provided by the complex, global capitalist system.[13] My neighbor's plight is the result of a long process by which social continuity has been sacrificed. Economic necessity demands social mobility.

## Quantity over Quality

Let us now look at the elevation of quantity over quality, using my own profession, higher education, as an example. Scholarship has always been valued in institutions of higher learning, though some civilizations (e.g.,

Confucian China) have given greater honor to scholars than others (e.g., the United States). In the United States, however, in the latter part of the twentieth century, a phenomenon known as "publish or perish" has pervaded higher education. The professor's promotion and tenure has become increasingly dependent on the number of publications produced per year; this number is reported in a bureaucratic procedure known as "the annual report." I recall a memo sent out by the president of my own university in the middle 1970s asking each department to elaborate formal criteria for promotion and tenure of faculty members, including quantitative criteria for scholarly production. There was no mention in the memo of the quality of what was produced except in a footnote! I do not think my own university was in any way unusual in this regard. At the end of one century and the beginning of another, workload issues have become increasingly important with regard to teaching on college campuses, with professors being closely monitored so that the number of hours taught by colleagues within a department are absolutely equal, but with little regard for the quality of the teaching or the overall contribution of a faculty member to the university. Previously, teaching fewer courses in one's own department meant the professor was engaging in other worthy outside activities (e.g., lecturing in other departments, serving on committees, directing interdisciplinary programs, and raising funds for such programs). Again, quantity of production was elevated over quality of service. In a completely different cultural setting, rural Jordan, I have observed the same tendency to elevate quantitative and often bureaucratic criteria over quality of learning. During my first anthropological fieldwork trip in 1959 to a village in Jordan where I conducted an ethnographic study, I met Luqman, the preacher of the village. Because I was interested in religion, specifically Islam, I attended his weekly mosque sermons and read the Quran with him for a full year. I gained a great deal of respect for his learning: he had amassed a considerable library of books on religion, gave people wise counsel on religious matters, and soon became a marriage officer and religious guide for the annual pilgrimage to Mecca. All this was accomplished without any formal religious education—Luqman, who had only a primary school education, learned from peripatetic preachers who spent brief periods in the district and the village. Luqman's father had insisted he drop out of the state school and go to work plowing the family lands after the sixth grade.[14] Informal learning in the home of the teacher or student and reading on one's own from one's own gradually developed library was the old mode of religious learning, and Luqman excelled at it. When I returned to the village in 1986 for an extended research trip, I discovered that there were a number of preachers in the region who had graduated from a two-year preacher's college set up by the central government in the late 1970s (there were very few preachers in the district in 1959). They were posted to various villages in the district and received a stipend from the government, depending on their educational degrees. They met once a week in the district office of the director of religious endowments to discuss various religious books pertaining to Islam and their preaching mission. Luqman was among them, although he was the only one to have been taught outside the formal classroom setting. The director wished to appoint one of the preachers as a special aide to oversee the selection of various lower-echelon mosque employees such as muezzins (callers-to-prayer) and suggested Luqman as the appropriate choice. No one demurred, but later in Luqman's absence the preachers angrily criticized the director's decision, saying that Luqman did not have a degree, he was not a product of the teacher's college, and his knowledge was backward and inferior (to their own). The director displayed surprise and annoyance; he said that it was true that Luqman did not have their formal education, but his self-taught knowledge amounted to a master's degree (i.e., was superior to their own). It was clear that the new generation of preachers measured learning quantitatively and bureaucratically, in terms of degrees that carried with them government stipends that measured scholarly worth!

## Commercial Efficiency over Human Sympathy

Finally, let us consider the evaluation of commercial efficiency (production and profit) over human sympathy for traditional values. The personal and human qualities that are undermined in the ideology of modernism deserve attention. Time plays an important role here. Two

7

political scientists, Lloyd and Susanne Rudolph, pointed out the similarity of Gandhi's daily schedule to Benjamin Franklin's in a book on political development in India.[15] Both men segmented the day's activities according to clock time, stipulating beginning and ending times for meals, bath, exercise, rest, study, sleep, and worship. Indeed, Gandhi was the more "modern" of the two, the more efficient and specialized in dividing activities by the clock, stipulating fourteen activities, beginning at 4 A.M. and ending at 9 P.M., whereas Franklin stipulated eleven, beginning at 5 A.M. and ending at 10 P.M. Modern life is clock-conscious life; the clock rules the day and cannot be ignored.

I cannot help remembering in this regard my first anticipated Quranic lesson with Luqman in 1959. We agreed that I would meet with him in his home to read the Quran every Wednesday at 2 P.M. I very much looked forward to the lesson. But the mayor of the village came to me a few days later and said he would like to take me to meet the leaders of another village in the vicinity on Wednesday. I said I would like to go with him, but I had arranged with the preacher to read the Quran with him at 2 P.M. The mayor said, "Oh, we'll go in the morning on horseback and return in plenty of time for your lesson." I agreed, provided he was sure we would return on time. He said, "Of course." We arrived in the other village early enough, around 10 A.M. Our host, an elder of the village, was delighted at our arrival and offered us tea, and we discussed various local matters, but very few men were available because they were all out in the fields plowing. It got to be just before noon, and I became anxious to leave in time to make my lesson. The mayor said, "Oh no, we can't leave now, our host has slaughtered a goat in your honor, and we will eat a grand meal when all the men return from the fields. Besides, it would be an affront to our host to leave now." I said, "I don't care, I have to leave," and I abruptly got up. The mayor was astonished and angry, and our host was perplexed and more than annoyed, for I was about to cost him an expensive meal and a loss of (animal) capital without a return in prestige. But I insisted, and we left. We arrived back in the village just before 2 P.M., and I rushed to Luqman's house and knocked on the door. His wife opened it and said that Luqman had gone on business to the next village. I replied anxiously, "But what about our lesson?" "Oh, you can have it tomorrow or the next day," she said; "the preacher is always around." Indeed he was, and we did read and complete the Quran, though not always at the appointed time. The point here is not that the preacher and other villagers lacked a sense of time. They had a good sense of ecological time: they knew exactly when to plow, plant, weed, and harvest. They had a good sense of ritual time: they prayed at all the appropriate worship periods on a daily basis. If they went into town, they knew when the markets were open or closed; and if they worked in an office or factory, they knew if they were consistently late they would be fired. But they were not bound by the clock and the call of efficiency, production, and profit.

The modern way of life submerges the important interpersonal ties that have bound societies together for thousands of years. Among these are ties of friendship. I recall many years ago being a visiting professor in the department of anthropology and sociology at the American University of Beirut, where a Lebanese colleague and I became good friends, eating meals together, visiting one another in off-work hours, and going on trips together in the Lebanese countryside. Late one morning he came to me as I was in the midst of preparing a class lecture I was to give in an hour's time, saying, "Let's go out for a cup of coffee and a smoke of the hubble-bubble pipe." I replied, "I'm sorry, Fuad, I have to finish preparing my lecture." Although I noted that Fuad was disappointed, I thought little about the matter. A few weeks later Fuad was busy preparing a lecture for a class he was to give in an hour's time, when his friend, a Lebanese professor, came in and said, "Fuad, let's go out for a cup of coffee and a hubble-bubble smoke." He replied, "Okay, let's go." This incident demonstrates that I was tied to the clock and my obligation to produce a lecture. Fuad was a good teacher and an excellent scholar, but he placed human sympathy and friendship first.

Also among these human ties are patron–client ties.[16] These ties are often discussed in a political or economic context, but such a discussion misses their human texture. During this same time (when I was a visiting professor in Beirut), I often had my shoes shined because of the dusty thoroughfares of a bustling entrepôt and because it was appropriate to my status in that university milieu. Outside the university gate there were six or seven men lined up next to one another who shined shoes.

Fortuitously, I chose one on the occasion of my first shoe shine; thereafter, that same man would always preempt the others and shine my shoes. Soon, he and I took it for granted that we were linked in a patron–client relationship. He always said he would give me a better shine than the others would, and I think he did because, over time, we developed a less instrumental and more personal relationship. Customarily, when I finished my shoe shine and went into the Lebanese restaurant opposite the gate, I experienced a similar relationship: the same waiter always came to serve me at the table, and every other patron of the restaurant had his or her own special waiter who offered superior service and jocular company.

These interpersonal ties that informed the ethos of a premodern society are being diminished, even in the rural areas of Jordan. Before the 1970s the prevailing custom in the villages of the Al-Kura district where I've done my research was that villagers who returned to the community after a long absence (six months to a year) always brought gifts for their close kinsmen. In this society this could mean a fairly large number of cousins, uncles, and aunts as well as immediate family members. And these close kinsmen reciprocated by inviting the returned villager to their homes for a sumptuous meal, sometimes involving the slaughter of an animal. In the 1970s and 1980s transnational migration from the village of Kufr al-Ma, where I conducted my research, to seventeen different countries for the purposes of work, higher education, and military training became common. Many villagers were coming and going with a frequency never before known. Now, they could not afford to bring gifts every time they returned, for they wished to save their money for their education, for the education of their children, or for commercial enterprises that they might start in the village and its environs with their savings from working abroad. And yet these returned villagers still expected their close kinsmen to invite them for meals or at least invite them to their homes as they had always done in the past. On their side, the kinsmen who remained in the village still expected their relatives to bring them gifts from abroad. There was disappointment of expectations on both sides. A new ethos had begun to replace the old one, which was composed of hospitality, cordiality, and mutual affection. Villagers characterized the new ethos for me by the Arabic term *mujamala*, which means politeness, but false politeness motivated by self-interest. That is, your kinsmen only visit you now because they want something from you, not because they have affection for you. Many close kinsmen no longer visit one another in a spontaneous fashion as was common; they will only come with a formal invitation, something unheard of in the village in 1959.

What does this discussion and all these examples have to do with fundamentalism? It is simply this: fundamentalism is a reaction, both ideological and affective, to the changes in basic social relationships that have occurred on a worldwide basis as a result of the social organizational, technological, and economic changes introduced by the modern world and as a result of the historical shift in power relations that has occurred over the last two hundred years in that world.

## The Historical Shift in Power Relations

The changes described in interpersonal terms above are part of a major historical shift in worldview and power relations that the historian of religion Bruce Lawrence, following Fernand Braudel, Marshall Hodgson, and Barrington Moore, has termed, "the Great Western Transmutation," hereafter referred to as GWT.[17] The GWT began at the end of the eighteenth century in western Europe and changed the outlook of human beings toward the material world. As a result of the Enlightenment, the French Revolution, the commercialization and industrialization of life, and the scientific revolution, a worldview that had been preoccupied with moral and ultimate questions (such as the quest for salvation) became preoccupied with puzzle solving in a world of expanding markets and opportunities. This was a world whose primary beneficiaries were the relatively few bankers, merchants, and politicians of western Europe. God's world was this new world and not the next world, and the work of this world was God's work, whereas before the work of this world was to prepare for the hereafter.[18] The GWT undermined the organic worldview that placed each class in its proper place for the length of the life cycle, it kicked off a revolution of rising expectations as to what could be achieved on this earth in this life, and it eventually led to the pluralization of private beliefs and the relativization of public values. That is, by the end of the twentieth century in the technologically advanced countries of the western world, public disagreement and debate about major social questions (e.g., abortion, unemployment, the impact of television, transnational migration, euthanasia) is accepted by the great majority of the population as normative, (i.e., as expected, desired, and routine). "I don't agree with you, but you've got the right to your opinion," or to put it another way, "Live and let live," is the dominant ethos accompanying this worldview. During the GWT, nationalism, liberalism, socialism, and civil religion (the belief in a creator God but not in specific religious creeds) become the dominant ideologies along with the overarching ideology of modernism.[19]

But the GWT that unfolded in the nineteenth century and continued through the twentieth century had a critical political dimension: It divided the world between winners and losers. The bureaucratization and technicalization of violence that began with the French Revolution and the Napoleonic wars—national conscription, ministries of defense, and the increasing sophistication and destructiveness of weaponry—and whose classic symbol in the twentieth century is the Pentagon, first produced the great European powers, then eliminated many of them, then eliminated the Third World, and finally eliminated all powers but one. Lawrence has pointed out that before the French Revolution, there were only ten world powers, based on their ability "to prepare for war, wage war, and win war."[20] Although he does not list them, they were England, France, Russia, Austria–Hungary, Holland, Spain, Portugal, Sweden, Prussia, and the Ottoman Empire. All but one, the Ottomans, were European. After World War I only six world powers, judged by their ability to wage modern war, existed: England, Italy, the United States, Russia, China, and Japan. By the end of World War II only two powers remained, the United States and the Soviet Union. And many have argued that after the Gulf War only one remains, the United States. The significant factor here is marginalization: fewer and fewer nations are able to compete effectively in the international arena; that is, relative political deprivation has become an increasing fact of the modern world. And although political deprivation and economic deprivation are not synonymous, they are clearly related. Political power can be converted into economic resources as Great Britain with its dominant sea power demonstrated through its colonial empire. And Japan's economic power has been converted into political power in the latter part of the twentieth century as its presence in world councils indicates.

In this national marginalization, generally speaking, Africans, Asians (excluding Japanese and Koreans), and Latin Americans have lost out. But the GWT has produced marginalization within nations—including European countries and the United States—as well as between them. For instance, at the end of the twentieth century in Germany and France, there were large numbers of transnational migrants who contributed critically to the economies of these nations, who were permanent residents, and whose children were born there, who exist in poverty. In the United States urban ghettos housed a substantial proportion of poor people in a population with a large middle class in an economy that was generally robust. Appalachia continued to be marginal economically and politically to the rest of the country.

With the "transnationalization of advanced capitalism," not only has the gap between the rich and the poor widened, but also "thanks to the airplane, the bus, [and] the truck, inequality and misery is in all senses closer to privilege and wealth than ever before."[21] Unlike previous centuries, migration in the twentieth century was not outward to peripheries in the New World, but "inwards towards the metropolitan cores."[22] As a result, the sense of relative deprivation grew more intense and personal. What are the implications of relative political and economic marginalization for fundamentalism? Fundamentalism is inherently oppositional and minoritarian. It is the protest of those *not* in power. Power here means political power, not necessarily economic power. Indeed, in the United States and Latin America it can be argued that fundamentalists are not the poor, but rather those who come from modest economic origins who are upwardly mobile. It is precisely the upwardly mobile who feel most sharply differences in power. They experience "relative" powerlessness in a pervasive manner.[23] In the Islamic case, fundamentalism has specifically arisen in the colonial context of political and economic domination and marginalization of colonized peoples. This

13

marginalization is not only political and economic, but because of the flooding of mass-produced goods into nonwestern markets as well as western-packaged ideas through the mass media, it is cultural as well. In the Christian case in the United States, marginalized classes and regions have persisted and grown along with prosperity. Indeed, prosperity and marginalization are interconnected because all do not benefit equally from the proliferation of opportunities in the global economy.

I do not wish to argue for a moment that fundamentalism can be explained through some simple correlation of economic and political power. "Deprivation" and "powerlessness" are matters of perception and are often symbolic constructions rather than reflections of material differences, but this fact does not make them any less "real." There is no question, however, that the thrust of world history—since the Congress of Vienna in 1815 through the Treaty of Versailles in 1919 to the Gulf War in 1991—has been the elimination of many formerly "first-class" nations into second- and third-class status and the political and symbolic marginalization of many groups within these nations.

## The Enemy As the Secular Nation-State

A special aspect of fundamentalist movements' protest against modernism is their protest against secular nationalism and the secular nation-state. Mark Juergensmeyer has argued that the secular nationalism that developed after the French Revolution had as its aim the replacement of loyalty to one's religious tradition or institution with loyalty to secular nationalism and the secular nation-state.[24] The rise of secular nationalism constituted an assault on religion. John Locke and Jean-Jacque Rousseau located the legitimacy of the nation-state in the people and not the church. Secular nationalism is based on the idea that the legitimacy of the state is based on the will of the people and not on religion or ethnic nationalism.[25]

As it developed in the nineteenth and twentieth centuries, nation-state loyalty was based on the ideology of nationalism, which was composed of four elements: a secular political ideology; a religiously neutral national identity (reflected in the United States by the doctrine of separation of church and state); a particular form of political organization (representative democracy); and an emotional identification with a geographic area and loyalty to a particular people.[26]

Secular nationalism, like religion, is also a framework for a moral order that justifies violence and martyrdom. Secular nationalism and religion, Juergensmeyer argues, are "competing ideologies of order."[27] Religion deals with problems of disorder and its theologies specifically assert and restore order both at the individual and group level.

In the nineteenth and twentieth centuries in the United States and Europe, religion was pushed to the periphery of societal concern, and elements of it were co-opted by nation-states in such modes as "civil religion."[28] That is, reference to God (but not specific creeds or prayers) was made a regular part of nation-state ritual (e.g., at the swearing in of American presidents or at state proclamations at Thanksgiving).[29] The assertion of religious nationalism (fundamentalism) was a defiant reaction to the co-optation and the watering down of religion by the nation-state to affirm its own societal legitimacy. From a fundamentalist perspective, nation-states had betrayed religious belief and practice by ignoring their core elements.

Juergensmeyer argues that the aim of religious nationalists was and is to relink religion to the nation-state. He also argues that modern religious protest movements differ from previous movements in that they are specifically aimed at the nation-state and its assertion of secular rather than religious legitimacy, civil religion being a frill rather than any serious religious involvement.[30] These modern religious protest movements reject secular nationalism; regard it as western and neocolonial; wage their struggle with religious rhetoric, ideology, and leadership; and offer a religious alternative to the secular nation-state—the religious nation-state.[31] These religious protest movements regard western culture and western governments as failures in their inability to realize their professed values (e.g., equality and social justice), and as failures in terms of their realization of the values that nonwestern societies regard as important: family stability, sobriety, societal order, and respect for the honor of women and men. The movements point to the high rates of divorce, out-of-wedlock births, alcoholism, drug abuse, crime, and the prevalence of pornography in these western societies as evidence for this failure.[32] From this perspective the secular nation-state has lost its legitimacy. The Iranian revolution against the Shah of Iran and his secular monarchy is an excellent example of this orientation and its successful application in the political arena. "Westoxification" (the falling of Iranian society under the pervasive influence of a corrupt western culture during the Shah's rule) was one of the persuasive charges made by religious militants in their successful campaign to overthrow the Shah's secular autocracy (see chapter five).

In the Middle East and South Asia, however, religion was and is so intimately woven into societal and political life that it was and is difficult to dislodge, even by the powerful nation-state. Moreover, many religious leaders in the western world as well as in Asia and the Middle East have such a deep distrust of secular nationalism and the nation-state that they spurn political engagement with it, whether in attempts to confront the state, capture it, or just to influence its policies.

In the chapters that follow we will examine not only those fundamentalist movements that engage the state and confront it (chapter five), but also those that seek to remain autonomous, to preserve their purity, and to build their own religious utopias (chapter four). The latter include the supporters of Bob Jones University in South Carolina, the *haredim* (ultraorthodox) of Jerusalem, and the members of the Society of Muslims, popularly known as "Excommunication and Flight" in Cairo, Egypt.

## The Cultural Content of Fundamentalism

This book argues that the worldview and ethos of fundamentalism is the same across cultures but that the cultural content and the historical circumstances of its emergence are not. This is an important point and if it is not understood from the beginning, much that follows will be misunderstood. The worldview of fundamentalism places God and his sacred scriptures, as well as the struggle of good and evil, at the center of both individual and group concern. Its ethos is one of minoritarian protest and outrage at the progressive displacement of religion from one institution after another in an increasingly secularized society. All fundamentalists share this worldview and ethos.

However, the cultural content of fundamentalism and the historical circumstances of its emergence (as well as its particular targeted opponents) differ substantially. The catalyst for the growth of Christian fundamentalism has been the growth and dominance of "progressive, patriotic Protestantism," a phrase coined by the historian Henry May to describe the development of a dominant American national religion by the end of the nineteenth and beginning of the twentieth century.[33] This religious ideology wedded the belief in secular progress to the view that it was America's God-given destiny to expand territorially and grow demographically and economically. Peculiar American institutions such as the free school, the Christian mission, and representative government were established by divine providence. Protestanism's salvation by faith and belief in the open Bible (open to reading and interpretation) and the priesthood of all believers found an extension and parallel in the belief that American democracy was part of the divine plan. May argues that the dominant preachers of this national faith were statesmen such as Theodore Roosevelt and Woodrow Wilson (the son of a minister) and not ministers in churches.[34] At the end of the nineteenth century American fundamentalists began mounting attacks on this national faith precisely because it elevated nationalism and secularism to the level of religion and because the struggle of God and Satan became submerged and replaced by the notion of progress (i.e., perfectibility on this earth). As immigrants poured into the country at the turn of the century, fundamentalists denounced threatening foreign cultural influences such as German kultur, the Catholic Church, and Bolshevism. They addressed the sociomoral crisis: the decline of the Bible as a guide, the change of sexual morality, and the decline of political morality as well as the decline of the family through the drive for women's emancipation. They endorsed work as a prophylactic against sin and warned of the approaching millennium in which all humankind would be judged by a stern and righteous God. After their success in getting the Eighteenth Amendment passed prohibiting the production and sale of alcoholic beverages just after World War I, fundamentalists began to attack the doctrine of evolution with renewed vigor as they had earlier attacked the German academic tradition of the "higher criticism" of the Bible.[35] From an early period, evolution had become a central focus of American Christian fundamentalism.

Although progressive, patriotic Protestantism and a response to the growing tide of immigration form the broad context of the growth of Christian fundamentalism in the United States at the end of the nineteenth and beginning of the twentieth century, its particular context and catalyst was narrower. Its particular catalyst and focus was the controversy over biblical interpretation and particular points of theological difference with other denominations over such matters as the timing of the millennium and the second coming of Christ, matters that split Protestant denominations in the late 1800s and early 1900s.[36]

Islamic fundamentalism, on the other hand, is driven by outrage at western cultural and economic penetration—not simply military and political control—as a result of western colonialism. From a Muslim perspective, the achievement of political independence by Muslim countries after World War II did not end colonialism. Most Muslims simply exchanged masters, the westernized Muslim elites for the European colonialists. Indeed, the neocolonial cultural and economic domination was felt to be more oppressive than the old politico-military domination. The galling cultural and economic domination of Moroccans by foreigners in an "independent Morocco" was expressed by a Muslim fundamentalist to an anthropologist in the 1970s when he said:

> the Fassis [urbanites of Fez] and the other rich Moroccans have forgotten their religion. They have become like Christians. Sometimes they speak French among themselves. They send their children to French schools. They marry French women. And even their Muslim wives and daughters bare their bodies like Christian whores. They wear bikinis at the beach and short skirts and low-cut blouses in the streets.[37]

In Morocco and other Muslim countries, fundamentalists interpreted this alien cultural and economic domination as a sign of the wrath of God and a call for the return to the Quran and strict adherence to its principles. They believed that this return to the Quran was necessary to achieve salvation in the darkness of a sinning and secularized world.

Interestingly enough, the sudden influx of wealth to Muslim elites in the Arabian Gulf and to North African countries that benefited from the 1973 and 1980 Organization of Petroleum Exporting Countries (OPEC) oil price increases has not resulted in a reduction in the feeling of powerlessness or a decrease in resentment against western economic and cultural control.[38] The quadrupling of oil prices resulted in the spectacular enrichment of the political and economic elites of these countries as opposed to the modest amelioration of the majority of the Muslim population, thereby accentuating feelings of relative deprivation by that majority. Although wealth poured into the countries of the Arabian Gulf in the 1970s and 1980s and numerous improvements of infrastructure were made, this influx of wealth had the paradoxical effect of dramatizing the inability of that elite to manage and maintain that infrastructure and its related institutions. They were not able to maintain and manage schools, roads, banks, hospitals, and factories. The elite had to call in thousands of foreigners (mainly Europeans and North Americans) to manage the institutions created by the new wealth, and they remain there to this day. Oil did not assuage feelings of domination and inferiority; rather it exacerbated them and strengthened the support for the fundamentalist attack on westerners and neocolonialism.

Jewish fundamentalism is not driven by outrage at colonialism or antipathy to evolution and positivist science.[39] It is driven by outrage at the virulent anti-Semitism that prevailed in many parts of eastern and central Europe in the late nineteenth and twentieth centuries. It is driven by official discrimination and persecution of Jews, and in the middle of the twentieth century by the outrage at the systematic program of genocide perpetrated by the Nazi regime in Germany, often with the toleration of the gentile world. In its nineteenth-century European origins, Jewish fundamentalism was perhaps even more a response to religious modernism and to the changes within the Jewish community including the Jewish enlightenment, the reform movement, secularization, and the rise of Zionism.[40] The Zionist movement and the establishment of the state of Israel in 1948 was the secular, nationalist reaction to European anti-Semitism. Jewish fundamentalism is the religious reaction to anti-Semitism and to its twentieth-century culmination in the Nazi Holocaust. Jewish fundamentalism in both Israel and the United States is also a reflection of the ambivalent relationship religious Jews have had to living in the diaspora, the lands outside historic Israel. In particular, in Europe it was a reaction to and a protest against the Enlightenment, nationalism, and the secularization of society including the assimilation of Jews into the national societies of western Europe in the late nineteenth and early twentieth centuries. Some Jewish fundamentalists, like most Christian fundamentalists, have accommodated to the State and accepted it as a means to accelerate the first stage of redemption (e.g., the movement of *Gush Emunim* [Bloc of the Faithful] in Israel).[41] However, other Jewish fundamentalists continue to regard the secular state as an enemy, like most Muslim fundamentalists, and to seek to separate themselves from secular society and the secular state.[42]

The above capsule account has described the quite different historical circumstances surrounding the rise of Christian, Islamic, and Jewish fundamentalism. What all these religious movements have in common is a protest against modernity; that is, the life ushered in by the GWT—bureaucratization, rationalization, technicalization, global exchange, and the relativization of public values and the pluralization of private beliefs. And what they all oppose vehemently is the accompanying ideology and ethos that enshrines change over continuity, quantity over quality, and consumer-oriented capitalism over human sympathy for traditional values. It remains to discuss the social composition of fundamentalist movements.

## Who Are the Fundamentalists?

Precisely who the fundamentalists are, socially, depends on what fundamentalist movement is discussed at what time in modern history and from what particular perspective. Five perspectives and one example are presented here. They are not presented to endorse any or all of them as the "right" view of the composition of fundamentalist movements. This would not be possible, in any case, because although they agree on some matters, they disagree on others. However, each view highlights certain aspects of fundamentalist recruitment that deserve attention.[43] Henry Munson, an anthropologist, has categorized fundamentalists in terms of a worldview that sees them choosing God's side in the ongoing and pervasive struggle of good against evil (Satan).[44] Fundamentalists differ among themselves in whether they regard this struggle as moral (with imperialism as a punishment for an immoral people) and as necessitating a strict return to the sacred scripture (Quran) or whether they see the struggle as political as well as moral and as necessitating not only moral reformation and a struggle against the oppressor but also the establishment of an Islamic state. In his application of this view of fundamentalism to Morocco in the 1970s and 1980s, Munson distinguishes three types of fundamentalists depending on the degree to which they regard the struggle as moral (focusing on a strict Islamic way of life including proper ritual and modest dress) or political (attacking imperialism and corrupt monarchy) as well. The types form a continuum ranging from most moral to most political as follows: traditionalistic, mainstream, and radical ideological fundamentalism.[45] Implicit in these categorizations is the distinction between "religious" and "religious-minded" people. These terms make a distinction between those people who most take their beliefs for granted (i.e., who spontaneously experience religion [the traditionalistic]) and those who are self-conscious in defense of their beliefs (i.e., who feel most threatened by outsiders [radical ideologists]).[46] It is interesting that two of the three fundamentalist leaders of the movements discussed by Munson were former inspectors in the ministry of education and the third was a Quran teacher. Also worth mentioning is that the supporters of the more political of these movements were students and members of the educated middle class among the with very few supporters peasants, workers, or people who migrated to cities from rural areas.

Bruce Lawrence, a historian of religion, has emphasized that in its leadership and core following, fundamentalism is a movement of secondary-level male elites.[47] These males, interestingly enough, are dominantly laymen, not clergy.[48] He notes that two prominent Muslim fundamentalist leaders in Pakistan, Abul-'Ala Mawdudi and Asrar Ahmed, were a jounalist and a medical doctor, respectively, before turning their attention to religious reform; and two other prominent Egyptian Muslim fundamentalists, Hassan al-Banna and Sayyid Qutb were, respectively, a teacher and a bureaucrat in the Ministry of Education. And Juhayman ibn Sayf al-'Utayba, who led the violent military takeover of the sacred mosque enclosure in Mecca in 1979, an audacious challenge to the Saudi state, was a soldier in the Saudi National Guard before he became a self-taught Muslim theologian.[49] In the United States Pat Robertson is by training a lawyer, and James Dobson is an educational psychologist, and although Jerry Falwell was trained in the ministry, he makes his living as a talk-show host. That is, fundamentalists are very much men of the world in the world. In Egypt in the 1980s Lawrence records that Muslim fundamentalists often came from upwardly mobile educated middle-class backgrounds and not from the dispossessed and downtrodden. In Saudi Arabia, Malaysia, and Iran in the late 1970s they came from the petite bourgeoisie; that is, from "marginalized out-of-power groups," and "estranged urban dwellers who continue to have attachment to rural roots and premodern values."[50] The male elites that led Muslim fundamentalist movements in this period and that would lead in the next decade were scientifically and professionally oriented, usually educated in western or Middle Eastern secular universities. Quite often, they were unemployed or underemployed "frustrated engineers, disaffected doctors, or unpaid bureaucrats in meaningless public jobs."[51] Lawrence's description of the social composition of Muslim fundamentalist movements affirms its diversified social base.

Martin Riesebrodt, a sociologist, compares the social composition of Protestant fundamentalists in the United States in the period from 1910 to 1928 with Shi'ah Muslim fundamentalists in Iran in the period from 1961 to1979 and finds some remarkable similarities.[52] Riesebrodt argues that fundamentalists are neither a class nor a dislocated amorphous mass. Rather, they are segments of different classes sharing the same experience and reacting to it through the same set of religious symbols or, alternatively, segments of society having different experiences that are expressed and reacted to through the same set of religious symbols.[53] He identifies fundamentalists with a particular "sociomoral milieu," meaning with a social movement whose members tend to share a number of attributes such as religion, regional tradition, economic position, and cultural orientation. This milieu is organized through voluntary religious associations that bring together previously separated people who share a certain worldview.[54] These people are brought together symbolically through a common set of images and ideas and often socially as well in a religious context. Riesebrodt also argues that fundamentalism is an urban protest movement recruited from all classes but featuring urban migrants, the traditional middle class, the clergy, and "border-crossers."[55] Border-crossers prominently include youth and white-collar bureaucrats. They are individuals of rural origins who come to the city, have received a secular education, and are thus alienated from many aspects of rural culture, but they are not modern in their worldview or ethos (e.g., they have conservative views of women and their dress, demeanor, and participation in public life including education and work).

In Iran in the prerevolutionary period (1963–1979), fundamentalist leaders were not usually avant-garde religious laypersons advocating social change (there were such leaders in Iran) but rather clergy who recruited followers in terms of personal patron–client relationships. That is, followers of particular religious leaders in particular regions sought their advice and counsel on a face-to-face basis and their economic support for the building of local schools, mosques, and hospitals. In return followers paid regional leaders an annual tithe and showed political support for them in marches, rallies, and demonstrations during the revolutionary period.[56]

Riesebrodt points out that in the United States fundamentalism also was an urban phenomenon, arising and flourishing in the large northern cities of New York, Chicago, Philadelphia, Boston, Baltimore, and Minneapolis as well as in Los Angeles.[57] The leaders of fundamentalist activity as well as the followership "came from confessions in which the conflict between modernism and orthodoxy was strongest, the Baptists and Presbyterians of the North."[58] Riesebrodt's demographic point is significant, not only because it challenges the stereotype of American fundamentalism as a rural and small-town phenomenon, but also because it focuses on rapid urbanization, industrialization, and mass migration. It was these processes that were transforming the United States from a personalistic and patriarchal (with family authority residing in the male head of

23

household) society to an impersonal and bureaucratic one, both in the communities and in the churches.[59] It is not accidental then that the invective of Protestant fundamentalists at the beginning of the twentieth century was xenophobic, citing "Rum and Romanism," and focusing on Roman Catholics and Jews. These were precisely the immigrant groups that were pouring into the northern cities where fundamentalism arose and, so the fundamentalists argued, they were eroding the moral values of the nation. The American South did not experience such mass immigration, rapid urbanization, or industrialization and did not participate as a core element in the fundamentalist protest movement until much later.

The organizers of the Protestant fundamentalist movement were pastors, evangelists, and lay preachers rather than theologians. That is, as with Muslim fundamentalists of the Middle East, the leaders were men involved in the day-to-day affairs of their congregations and classrooms or in conversion campaigns rather than thinkers set apart from society. Drawing on studies of the First Baptist Church of Minneapolis from 1903 to 1926, Riesebrodt notes that fundamentalists were drawn from all residential areas in the city, and appealed "to some well-to-do, and some poor, but also . . . to the 'respectable' Protestant and northern European working class."[60] In the 1920s a high percentage of the church's membership was composed of upwardly mobile urban migrants. Regarding higher education, contrary to the stereotype, Riesebrodt states that 75 percent of fundamentalist preachers in the 1920s had college degrees.[61]

Ian Lustick, a political scientist, has in one way broadened and in another way narrowed the application of the term fundamentalist by linking it to political activism. He defines fundamentalism as "a style of political participation characterized by unusually close and direct links between one's fundamental beliefs and political behavior designed to effect radical change."[62] Fundamentalists are identified by three attributes: uncompromisable injunctions, belief that their behavior is "guided by direct contact with the source of transcendental authority," and "political attempts to bring about rapid and comprehensive change."[63] By defining fundamentalism in this way, Lustick was able to identify *Gush Emunim* in modern Israel as a fundamentalist movement and to rule out other Jewish religious groups in Israel such as the *haredim* (ultra-orthodox Jews) as

and religious life with small meetings, overlapping groups, and frequent home visits. These low thresholds mean that "it is simple to organize a church and not very difficult to gain recognition as a religious leader. . . . The poorer the church, the more it depends on expansion to survive."[72]

Levine and Stoll argue that the focus is not on voluntary organizations, development agencies, church structures, or political or trade union organizations as much as on the "networks of trust, confidence, and organizational capacity" that arise out of the informal social relations described above.[73]

Finally, they argue that an essential component of the attraction of the new Protestant movements in Latin America is their evangelical character. Levine and Stoll define evangelical Protestantism in terms of three beliefs: the reliability on the Bible as a final authority; the necessity of being "born again" (i.e., of being "saved" as an adult through a personal relationship with Jesus Christ); and "the importance of spreading this message of salvation to every nation and person."[74]

## Father Luigi Giussani As an Example

To put a human face on fundamentalism, to demonstrate its complexity, and to indicate the way the term should and should not be taken in this book, I introduce an example of one fundamentalist leader and movement. Father Luigi Giussani is a parish priest in the industrial city of Milan in northern Italy. He founded two re-Christianization movements in and around Milan: Student Youth in the 1950s and Communion and Liberation in 1970. These movements aimed, as Giussani said, "to fight for the visible presence of the Church in a world where man has withdrawn far from God."[75] These movements were based on small groups at the local level sharing ritual and worship. They also sought to meet the needs of those "left by the wayside by modernization."[76] In Italy such people included the unemployed, student dropouts, and drug addicts during a period of Italian history rocked by economic depression, social dissension, and terrorism.[77] These movements provided mutual support networks, promoting integration of young people and the unemployed into the world of work.

Father Luigi Giussani is presented as an example of a fundamentalist here not because he typifies the social structural traits just listed above or the themes or attributes of fundamentalism discussed throughout the book. On the contrary, in some respects Father Giussani is quite atypical. First, he is a Roman Catholic. Most Christian fundamentalists are Protestants. Second, he is a clergyman. Fundamentalists are most often laymen. Third, between 1974 and 1989 Giussani and his Communion and Liberation Movement were looked on favorably by Pope John Paul II and were even said to be part of his "entourage."[78] Generally, fundamentalists are members of minoritarian movements (i.e., "outs" struggling against "ins," the political and religious establishments of their time). In this period Giussani and his movement were certainly not outs because they enjoyed the Pope's favor.

Yet in other respects Giussani's activity in northern Italy captures many fundamentalist themes. His Student Youth Movement drew inspiration solely from the scriptures. Scripturalism is a theme of this book. Although he is a clergyman, his followers are nearly all laymen. His activity was mainly in urban centers; fundamentalism's origin and present activity is largely urban. His Student Youth Movement was founded as a direct competitor of the established formal organization of the Catholic Church working with youth, Catholic Action. Student Youth was very much, then, an overt challenge to the established church. Furthermore, fundamentalists are often anticlerical and they operate outside regular worship centers. Student Youth bypassed diocesan and parish centers; that is, it bypassed the bishops and priests of the church. Members of the Communion and Liberation Movement were often critical of the members of the church hierarchy.

Giussani defined the enemy as secularism and, behind it, the Enlightenment that elevated reason above all things; Marxism was just the latest product of the Enlightenment.[79] Student Youth aimed at "breaking with the motivations and outlook of the 'dominant secularism' of the time."[80] The worldview of fundamentalism rejects the secular nation-state and repudiates secular values in society.

Finally, Giussani's movements were very much aimed at "action in the world" through two organizations, the Company of Deeds, which worked to give the unemployed jobs, and the People's Movement, which worked with the Christian Democratic Party (an establishment party) in various election campaigns. One prominent theme of fundamentalism is its activist—in this world—orientation.

The example of Father Luigi Giussani reflects the complexity of fundamentalism: his Student Youth Movement avoided the establishment church but his Communion and Liberation Movement worked hand and glove with it in many enterprises. At the same time they were working with the church, they openly criticized its leaders. In terms of the themes discussed in this book, Giussani's movements were both confrontational and separationist.

The example of Father Giussani makes one important point about fundamentalists and fundamentalism. They are ideal types, and no one individual or group is completely fundamentalist or completely lacking in fundamentalist attributes. Rather, in the real world in which individuals such as Father Giussani exist, a complex combination of attributes characterizes their action and beliefs.

Not all the definitions of fundamentalism or the distinctions between fundamentalists and others given above are mutually compatible. For instance, Lawrence would clearly include the *haredim* as fundamentalists because they are engaged in a strenuous protest against the modern world by their style of life and separatist social policy (some live in a particular quarter of Jerusalem and close the gates of the quarter on the Sabbath, not permitting anyone to exit or enter until the Sabbath ends). Lustick excludes them because they are not committed to militant political activity to achieve their goals. All that being said, Lustick and Lawrence *do* call attention to many prominent common attributes of fundamentalist movements: the focus on the struggle of good and evil; the male, lay character of its leadership; its centering on a changing urban milieu leading to religious protest; the informal, interpersonal character of its often wide-ranging networks of trust and confidence; and the militant political character of its activity. The remaining chapters of this book will dwell on the themes that unite most Christian, Jewish, and Muslim fundamentalists: the protest against change; the quest for purity; the search for authenticity, totalism, and activism; the necessity of certainty (scripturalism); selective modernization; and the centering of the mythic past in the present (including the concept of the covenant, the land, and the people).

## Notes

1. For a few references to the journalistic view of fundamentalists and fundamentalist-related institutions, events, and customs such as veiling, the treatment of women, congregational prayer, doctrinaire beliefs, fanaticism, and opposition to science, see the following: *Time* magazine covers for 26 November 1979, 7 January 1980, and 26 July 1982 for various menacing portraits of Ayatollah Khomeini; *New York Times Magazine* covers (and accompanying articles) on veiling in Jordan (12 December 1990) and Saudi Arabia (10 March 1991), which suggest the oppression of women and on Friday congregational prayer; the cover photograph accompanied by the cover title, "The Islamic Wave" (31 May 1992); and the magazine *Marie Claire*, April 1998, 50–56.

2. As quoted in Daniele Hervieu-Leger, "Faces of Catholic Transnationalism: In and Beyond France," in *Transnational Religion and Fading States*, ed. Susanne H. Rudolph and James Piscatori (Boulder, Colo.: Westview, 1997), 106. Other responses discussed by the author include a do-it-yourself approach to belief, the multiplication of transnational "mobile affinity networks," ecumenical networks, and the standardization of religious culture.

3. For an example of this argumentation, see Ilyas Ba-Yunus, "The Myth of Islamic Fundamentalism," *East-West Review* 1, no. 2, (1995): 58–75.

4. Bruce Lawrence, *Defenders of God* (San Francisco: Harper and Row, 1989), 93.

5. Most notably, by Benedict Anderson in his notable work, *Imagined Communities* (London: Verso, 1991).

6. Lawrence, *Defenders of God*, 93.

7. I am indebted here to the early work of the anthropologist Clifford Geertz, who made the distinction between worldview and ethos, the cognitive and the emotional, as the basis of his description and analysis of religion. See Geertz, "Ethos. World-View and the Analysis of Sacred Symbols," *Antioch Review* 17, no. 4 (December 1957), and "Religion as a Cultural System," in *Anthropological Approaches to the Study of Religion*, ed. Michael Banton (London: Tavistock, 1966) for Geertz's definition and usage of terms.

8. Paul Sigmund's definition as quoted in Lawrence, *Defenders of God*, 76.

9. Of course this statement is a generalization that has many exceptions (e.g., the prophets of the monotheistic religious traditions, Moses and Muhammad, led revolutionary religious movements, and the early Christianity of Jesus certainly had revolutionary implications, theologically, ideologically, socially, and politically).

10. Lawrence's full definition of modernism is as follows (*Defenders of God*, 27):

Modernism is the search for individual autonomy driven by a set of socially encoded values emphasizing change over continuity; quantity over quality; efficient production, power and profit over sympathy for traditional values or vocations, in both public and private spheres. At its utopian extreme, it enthrones one economic strategy, consumer-oriented capitalism, as the surest means to technological progress that will also eliminate social unrest and physical discomfort.

11. See William H. Whyte, *The Organization Man* (New York: Simon and Schuster, 1956).

12. See Gideon Sjoberg, *The Pre-Industrial City: Past and Present* (New York: The Free Press, 1960), for an account of preindustrial urban life in the major civilizations of Asia and the Middle East.

13. Interestingly enough, the rapid spread of personal computers may lead to a reuniting of home and work milieus with businesses run out of homes. What the social and individual human consequences of such reunification will be is unknown.

14. I have analyzed the sermons and the life of this preacher in terms of "the social organization of tradition"; that is, the process by which culture brokers such as the preacher (or teacher or judge or balladeer) pass on in a selective fashion their tradition, in the book, *Muslim Preacher in the Modern World* (Princeton, N.J.: Princeton University Press, 1989). See also my capsule analysis of the preacher's life, "Shaykh Luqman: A Contemporary Life in a Traditional Context," in *Windows on the House of Islam*, ed. John Renard (Berkeley: University of California Press, 1998).

15. See Lloyd and Susanne Rudolph, *The Modernity of Tradition: Political Development in India* (Chicago: University of Chicago, 1967), 223.

16. For an informed discussion of how patron–client ties operate in the Mediterranean and Middle East, see Ernest Gellner and John Waterbury, eds., *Patrons and Clients* (London: Duckworth, 1977).

17. See Lawrence, chapter two in *Defenders of God* for details.

18. Max Weber has argued that in Europe this shift in worldviews was also connected to the Protestant Reformation, in particular the Calvinist version of it. For his argument, see Weber, *The Protestant Ethic and the Spirit of Capitalism*, trans. Talcott Parsons (New York: Charles Scribner, 1958).

19. For a description and analysis of civil religion in the United States, see Robert Bellah's "Civil Religion in America," in *Beyond Belief: Essays on Religion in a Post-Traditional World*, ed. Robert Bellah (New York: Harper and Row, 1970).

20. Lawrence, *Defenders of God*, 50. See also Lawrence's discussion of the rise of the West in chapter two of *Defenders of God*.

21. As quoted in Benedict Anderson, chapter three in *The Spectre of Comparisons: Nationalism, Southeast Asia, and the World* (New York: Verso, 1998), 67.

22. Anderson, *The Spectre of Comparisons*, 67.

23. As an example, the French revolution was not led by the economically depressed classes, but rather by upwardly mobile successful lawyers such as Danton and Robespierre, who nevertheless felt relatively powerless because they were blocked from advancement by the prominence of the French nobility.

24. See Mark Juergensmeyer, *The New Cold War? Religious Nationalism Confronts the Secular State* (Berkeley: University of California, 1993) for the details of the argument. Juergensmeyer substitutes the phrase "religious nationalism" for fundamentalism, but the phenomenon he describes is essentially the same as described in this book.

25. Juergensmeyer, *The New Cold War?*, 11.

26. Juergensmeyer is following the definition of nationalism advanced by Hans Kohn and Rupert Emerson. See Juergensmeyer, *The New Cold War?*, 13–14.

27. Juergensmeyer, *The New Cold War?*, 30.

28. Juergensmeyer, *The New Cold War?*, 35.

29. See Bellah, "Civil Religion in America," for the details of the argument.

30. Juergensmeyer, *The New Cold War?*, 46.

31. Juergensmeyer, *The New Cold War?*, 46.

32. See John O. Voll's essay, "Islamic Renewal and the "Failure of the West" in Richard Antoun and Mary Hegland, eds., *Religious Resurgence: Contemporary Cases in Islam, Christianity, and Judaism* (Syracuse: Syracuse University, 1987) for an example of this fundamentalist perspective in the Islamic world.

33. See Henry May's essay, "The Religion of the Republic," in Henry May, *Ideas, Faiths and Feelings: Essays in American Intellectual and Religious History* (Oxford: Oxford University Press, 1983).

34. May, "The Religion of the Republic," 177–80.

35. The "higher criticism" was an attempt by scholars in the late nineteenth century, first in Germany and later in other European countries and the United States, to apply the principles of standard historical, critical analysis to the texts of the Bible. See Martin Riesebrodt, chapter two in *Pious Passion: The Emergence*

*of Modern Fundamentalism in the United States and Iran* (Berkeley: University of California Press, 1993), and Lawrence, chapter seven in *Defenders of God*, for brief analyses of the rise of fundamentalism in the United States.

36. I wish to thank the anonymous reviewer of an early draft of the book for making this point.

37. As quoted in Henry Munson, *The House of Si Abd Allah* (New Haven, Conn.: Yale University Press, 1984), 22. See Henry Munson's description of the differences between fundamentalist and mainline [the terms are mine] religious ideologies as represented in the views of the first cousins, Al-Hajj Muhammad and Fatma Zohra.

38. The Organization of Oil Producing Countries (OPEC) quadrupled the price of oil in 1973, thereby benefiting the economies of a number of Muslim countries in the Middle East including Libya, Algeria, Saudi Arabia, Kuwait, Iraq, Bahrain, and the United Arab Emirates.

39. Positivist science is wedded to the skeptical ethos that questions all things and never accepts any finding as final, in the sense that that finding is always subject to further experimentation and testing.

40. I wish to thank the anonymous reviewer of this book in its manuscript phase for making this point.

41. See Ian Lustick, *For the Land and the Lord: Jewish Fundamentalism in Israel* (New York: Council on Foreign Relations, 1988) for a penetrating description and analysis.

42. See Samuel Heilman, *Defenders of the Faith: Inside Ultra-Orthodox Jewry* (New York: Schocken Books, 1992), for a penetrating description and analysis of fundamentalists pursuing the separatist strategy.

43. The question of who fundamentalists are, socially, is different from the question of how fundamentalism is defined as a phenomenon in the modern world. The latter question has been addressed earlier in the chapter.

44. Munson, *The House of Si Abd Allah*, 20–21.

45. See Munson, chapter six in *Religion and Power in Morocco* (New Haven, Conn.: Yale University, 1993).

46. A distinction made by Geertz as quoted in Munson, *Religion and Power in Morocco*, 181.

47. Lawrence, *Defenders of God*, 100.

48. In this regard, Ayatollah Khomeini is the exception. Munson's ministry of education inspectors are more the rule.

49. Lawrence, *Defenders of God*, 195.

50. Lawrence, *Defenders of God*, 196.

51. Lawrence, *Defenders of God*, 197.

52. See Riesebrodt, *Pious Passion*, 1993.

53. Riesebrodt, *Pious Passion*, 26–28.

54. Riesebrodt, *Pious Passion*, 29.

55. See Riesebrodt, *Pious Passion*, 185–189.

56. For the details of this kind of patron–client relationship in a revolutionary and prerevolutionary context, see Michael Fischer, *Iran: From Religious Dispute to Revolution* (Cambridge: Harvard University, 1980). For a more general view of clergy–state relations in Iran in the prerevolutionary period, see Shahrough Akhavi, *Religion and Politics in Contemporary Iran* (Albany: State University of New York, 1980).

57. By the middle of the twentieth century the focus of fundamentalist strength and activity had shifted to the South and West where it remains today.

58. Riesebrodt, *Pious Passion*, 73.

59. See Riesebrodt, *Pious Passion*, chapter two for the details of the argument.

60. Marsden as quoted in Riesebrodt, *Pious Passion*, 82.

61. Riesebrodt, *Pious Passion*, 84.

62. Lustick, *For the Land and the Lord*, 5.

63. Lustick, *For the Land and the Lord*, 6.

64. Lustick, *For the Land and the Lord*, 7.

65. Lustick, *For the Land and the Lord*, 83.

66. Lustick, *For the Land and the Lord*, 11.

67. See Daniel H. Levine and David Stoll, "Bridging the Gap between Empowerment and Power in Latin America," in Rudolph and Piscatori, eds., *Transnational Religion and Fading States* (Boulder, Colo.: Westview Press, 1997), for details of the argument.

68. Levine and Stoll, "Bridging the Gap," 72.

69. Ibid.

70. Ibid.

71. Levine and Stoll, "Bridging the Gap," 73.

72. Ibid.

73. Ibid.

74. Levine and Stoll, "Bridging the Gap," 97. "Fundamentalist" and "evangelical" are overlapping categories. Many Christian fundamentalists are evangelicals and vice versa. In this book fundamentalists are defined by the presence of particular attributes (e.g., protest against the modern world, concern for purity, activism and totalism, scripturalism, the practice of "traditioning," and selective modernization). Evangelicals are distinguished by their view that Christians

must be "born again" (i.e., have a decisive religious experience as an adult that commits them to Jesus and to the religious life). Not all fundamentalists are evangelicals in this sense, and not all evangelicals share all the attributes of fundamentalism. For divergent views on this distinction, see Nancy Ammerman, *Bible Believers: Fundamentalism in the Modern World* (Piscataway, N.J.: Rutgers University Press, 1987) and Susan Harding, *The Book of Jerry Falwell: Fundamentalist Language and Politics* (Princeton, N.J.: Princeton University Press, 2000).

75. Gilles Kepel, *The Revenge of God: The Resurgence of Islam, Christianity and Judaism in the Modern World* (University Park, Penn.: Pennsylvania State University, 1994), 61. See also chapter two of *The Revenge of God*, "Mission Field Europe" for an account of the resurgent Christian movements founded in Italy by Father Guissani.

76. Kepel, *The Revenge of God*, 61.

77. See Kepel's discussion of these issues in *The Revenge of God*, 60–75.

78. Kepel, *The Revenge of God*, 70.

79. See Kepel, *The Revenge of God*, 62 for details.

80. Kepel, *The Revenge of God*, 67.

*Chapter Two*

# THE COMPLEXITY
# OF SCRIPTURALISM

Recent studies of fundamentalism by western scholars identify as one of its main attributes the literal belief in an inerrant sacred scripture as the word of God.[1] Literalism and inerrancy have been synonyms for the rigidity of fundamentalist thought. This focus, however, oversimplifies a very complex phenomenon. Scripturalism—the focus on religious scriptures— is important and central for fundamentalist thought and practice, but literalism and inerrancy are not its main attributes. Many fundamentalists claim to believe literally in the scriptures in their entirety, but many others do not.[2] Rather, it is the emotional and inspirational qualities of scripture, their relation to the numinous, their grounding of nationalism and nation-states, their use as proof-texts in the assertion of certainty and application to everyday life, their scandalous character, and their selective use that is important. Each of these aspects of scripture is discussed below.

## Numinous Experience, Inspirational and Emotional Qualities

Simply by reading and believing scripture, the religious person is transformed, inspired, and comforted. When the Moroccan Hajj Muhammad (see chapter four) goes to the mosque, "the white-washed walls and the chanting of the Quran wash away the sadness and all the worries of the world. I chant the Quran with the tulba [students]. And then we pray."[3]

Hajj Muhammad often chants the call to prayer, which is filled with Quranic phrases, "and this makes the sadness disappear:

> God is greater, God is greater
> I bear witness that there is no god but God
> I bear witness that there is no god but God
> I bear witness that Muhammad is the messenger of God
> I bear witness that Muhammad is the messenger of God
> Come alive to prayer
> Come alive to prayer
> Come alive to success
> Come alive to success
> God is greater
> God is greater
> There is no God but God
> When I hear the call to prayer, I go to the mosque by the stream. And there I feel happy and clean.[4]

The chanting of the Quran has such a powerful effect on Hajj Muhammad not because it stipulates a set of divine laws, but rather because it puts him in touch with the sacred. The Quran and Traditions of the Prophet (the second source of religious truth for Muslims after the Quran) have taken root among millions of Muslims, not because it was forced on them by rulers but because in the words of Karen Armstrong, it gave "men and women an experience of the numinous and imbue[d] their lives with meaning."[5] That is, it put them in touch with the divine and allowed them to acquire a sense of "interior submission" to that divine power.[6]

Another example of the inspirational quality of scripture comes from fundamentalist Christianity. In a 1923 debate in Calvary Baptist Church in New York City on the question, "Resolved that the Bible is the Infallible Word of God," more than 10,000 people witnessed as the fundamentalist preacher Reverend John R. Straton pointed to the transformative and uplifting influence of the Bible. He cited how many individuals who came "from lives of crime and shame" had their lives "made over" as a result of reading the Bible, which they delighted to quote to delineate the "truths [that] saved them."[7] Straton described a painting entitled *The Entrance of Thy Word Giveth Light*, which illustrated the power of the Bible:

The young man (from a poverty stricken home) lay upon the bed in the early morning after a night of drunkenness and debauchery. Beside him sat the venerable old mother of the wayward lad. A tear was upon her wrinkled cheek; the old family Bible was upon her open knee, and with her drawn, crooked finger she was tracing laboriously and reading the words of counsel and truth from the Book. And with marvelous spiritual insight and skill the artist had managed to suggest the dawn of hope upon the young man's face. Realizing his own weakness and his own inability to stand amidst the temptations of human life—convinced at last of his own moral impotence—there came to his penitent soul the revelation that there was another power, a Beneficent and Divine Power, that would strengthen his weak will and correct the sad abuses of his life, and so the entrance of God's word gave him light. That picture is true, and that experience has been repeated many million times upon our earth.

In the homes of Protestant fundamentalists, the worshiper's personal Bible (which in the days before municipal birth records, recorded the birthdays and death days of all family members) became a private interpersonal record of the trials and tribulations of each family member. It was often annotated in the margins of particular biblical verses with the reactions of concern or inspiration of the verse's reader, as he or she recited aloud or whispered the scripture, a reading tradition familiar to monotheism. Often the Bible was an emotional history of the family as well as a sacred text.

## Scripture As Proof-Texts

Particular verses of scripture serve as proof-texts for fundamentalists. That is, verses are recited in the middle of the flow of everyday life or in the midst of a discussion or debate and used to justify certain beliefs and practices. When I was conducting anthropological field work in the peasant village of Kufr al-Ma, Jordan, during the winter months I would often look up at the partly cloudy sky in the morning and ask a villager if he thought it was going to rain. He would often reply by reciting a verse from the Quran such as, "Hast thou not seen that God knows whatsoever is in the heavens, and whatsoever is in the earth" (58:7). Once when a villager and I were discussing our respective back problems, I commented that man had a pronounced tendency to have such problems because unlike the rest of animal creation who walked on four legs, man was a strange two-legged creature who stood upright behind the plow or, as hunter, ran on two feet after his prey. The villager, by way of refutation of my invidious comparison, immediately quoted the Quranic verse: "Surely we created man of the best stature" (95:4).[8] Scripture here is cited in a pragmatic way to explain and justify particular attitudes toward the weather and bodily ailments.

The Moroccan Hajj Muhammad's rejoinder to Europeans denigrating Islam as a primitive religion was to quote the verse of the Quran below, which affirmed that God was one. By direct inference, Christianity was the primitive religion since (from a Muslim perspective) it was polytheistic, worshiping three gods (i.e., the doctrine of the Trinity):

> In the name of God, the merciful, the compassionate
> Say He is the one God
> The Eternal God
> He has never begotten, nor was He begotten
> And there has never been anyone like Him[9]

And when Hajj Muhammad described the laborious and paltry life of charcoal-makers and urban labor migrants (of which he was one) in Morocco, a life that included paying fines and being jailed for charcoal collection, he quoted a verse of the Quran for solace and justification of his lot: "Verily God is with those who patiently endure."[10]

Bethany Baptist Academy is a Christian academy in Illinois that explicitly attempts to be a "total institution," which will encompass nearly all the students' world and cut them off from secular influence. This school policy is justified by reference to the biblical verse from 2 Corinthians 6:17: "Wherefore come out from among them, and be ye separate, saith the Lord, and touch not the unclean thing."[11]

This scriptural passage was addressed to the parents of students as much as the students themselves to emphasize the necessity of their guarding the mind and behavior of their children because, as one teacher put it, "the Christian life is a total life. It's not just eight hours of school."[12]

On the other hand, the proof-text that is often cited at the academy by teachers and students to justify the absolute necessity "to be born again" (i.e., to accept Jesus Christ as Savior as an adult and to testify in public to that belief in order to be identified as a true Christian) is John 14:6: Jesus said to Thomas, "I am the way, and the truth, and the life; no one comes to the Father but by me."[13]

## The Yearning for Certainty

The constant reference to the scriptures relates to the thirst for certainty in an ever-changing world. The onset of rapid change began with the Great Western Transmutation (see chapter one) and has accelerated ever since. By the beginning of the twentieth century, Americans certainly felt that change. In the early-century theological debate in New York City referred to above, the fundamentalist minister Straton expressed the yearning for authority and certainty:

Shall the highest interests of our natures be left to caprice and chance? Are we forever to grope in darkness and uncertainty? Are there no fixed standards? No solid and enduring ground on which we can build our individual lives, establish our homes, order our society and found our hopes of Heaven? Is each one of us to be left to believe one thing one day—and that thing perhaps different from everything our neighbors are believing,—and another thing tomorrow, and another thing the next day, and so on and on?[14]

Pastor Straton returned to the theme of certainty and authority later in the debate:

The rejection of authority in the civil state, in the home, in social life, and in the church is the greatest and most menacing danger of today. Half of the world has been already plunged into anarchy, and the other half seems trembling upon the brink of that dreadful precipice, because the truth of authority has been rejected by the superficial thinking of the times. In the home, parental authority has waned, and the result is the wreck and ruin which is falling already upon the younger generations.[15]

41

If this desire for authority and certainty was so strong at the beginning of the twentieth century, how much more so is it at the end of the twentieth and the beginning of the twenty-first? It is in this latter period that the mass media, above all cable television, have widely publicized the tragedies of public and private life, dwelling on episodes of school, urban, suburban, and domestic violence such as the shootings at Columbine High School in Colorado; the bombing of the federal building in Oklahoma City; and the bombing of the World Trade Center in New York City. It is in the last half of the twentieth century, after all, that the United States has fought four wars (although they may have been officially designated as international police actions): the Korean War, the Vietnamese War, the Gulf War, and the Yugoslav War over Kosovo. Add to these unsettling events the instability of the interconnected transnational economic system and the domestic repercussions of adjustments to the electronic age in which computerized services and chain stores are displacing small (often family-run) enterprises, disrupting the life of many communities. It is not strange that the quest for authority and certainty has been mightily reinforced.

Scripturalism meets this need for certainty and authority for many people and gives them confidence to continue their pursuits, often in situations where the odds are heavily against them. Scripturalism allows people to proceed in the face of adversity and often jeopardy when others without their faith do not.

A good example of the strength of such scriptural faith is Ayatollah Khomeini's defiance of the United States during the crisis set off by the taking of American hostages in Tehran during the Iranian revolution in 1979.[16] The hostages were held for more than a year as the crisis escalated and as first President Carter, then President Reagan threatened to martial the military and economic might of the United States against Iran and to crush it. When the Papal Legate, sent by Pope John Paul II to intercede with Ayatollah Khomeini to release the hostages, arrived in Tehran in November 1979, he was refused an audience with Khomeini, who finally delivered a statement to him that was widely published in the world press:

> Let me announce here that we are neither afraid of military interference nor are we afraid of economic siege, since we are Shi'ite (Muslims) and as

Shi'ites we welcome any opportunity for sacrificing our blood.[17] Our nation looks forward to an opportunity for self-sacrifice and martyrdom. Now let us suppose that in the absence of all reasoning Carter or perhaps the superpowers should agree to send military forces here. Well, then, we have a population of 35 million, most of whom long for martyrdom. We'll go to battle with all these 35 million people, and once we are all martyred, then our enemies can do whatever they want to do with this country. We are not afraid of such an encounter. We are men of war, we are born of struggle. Our youth have fought against army tanks and machine guns with their hands. Mr. Carter need not frighten us of any warlike encounter. We are men of war even though we may go into action without the equipment of war. Again, as for economic siege, let me remind you that we are a nation who has long been accustomed to starving. We have been involved in these [economic] bottlenecks for 25 or rather 50 years. If such should be the case, we will all fast.[18]

Khomeini's scripturalist faith—as an Islamic scholar he had written many books analyzing the Quran and the Traditions of the Prophet—enabled him to process the information he was receiving that nonfundamentalists would interpret as portending his destruction by a great world power, and to interpret it positively in terms of religious faith and readiness to sacrifice.

Two anthropologists, Gerlach and Hine, have referred to this process as "deviation amplification" to handle doubt.[19] That is, (scripturalist) religious faith expresses itself in an ideology that is able to absorb negative information and render it positive and confidence-inspiring. Khomeini converted a situation that most outside observers would have regarded as threatening to the nation-state of Iran and particularly to its religious leadership into a situation that inspired religious fervor and solidified national support.

Turning to the United States, the Concerned Women of America, who engaged in various legal battles to advance fundamentalist causes, reflect a similar scripturalist faith and ideology. When the organization suffers legal defeats, they are regarded as "God's greater plan." A leading member of the organization said after a recent legal defeat, "God did not put us here to win the battle. The battle is His. We are just the foot-soldiers. So if the school [health] clinic [which would spread promiscuity] does open, it is not because we lost, but because it is God's plan."[20] Scripturalism provides the needed emotional strength to proceed against the odds.

## The Scandalous Character of Scripturalist Passages

Two historians of religion, Martin Marty and Scott Appleby, have called attention to another aspect of scripturalism: "Fundamentalists consistently retrieve and stress those teachings or practices from the past which clearly do not 'fit' in an 'enlightened' and 'sophisticated' modern society."[21] Secularized Muslims, Christians, and Jews who are no longer comfortable with many of the doctrines and rituals based on the scriptures, regarding them as outmoded and superstitious, have them thrown in their faces by fundamentalists who regard them as the mark of a true believer. Christian fundamentalists stress the birth of Christ to the Virgin Mary, a doctrine that is, incidentally, accepted by Muslims, who recognize Mary's virginal state (though not Jesus' divinity) in a book of the Quran named "Maryam" (Mary). Another set of scandalous beliefs for many "modern" Christians is the belief in the "substitutionary blood atonement of Jesus,"[22] and his bodily resurrection from the grave where he appeared to five hundred, and forty days later ascended unto heaven. In the documentary film *Protestant Spirit U.S.A.*, a fundamentalist minister, preaching in the Baptist Temple in Indianapolis, Indiana, revels in answering his own rhetorical question, "Where is heaven? Heaven is up there on the right hand side past the atmosphere, past the stratosphere and well beyond our solar system."[23] He urges his congregation, "Make your reservations for heaven on this side of death" before it is too late.

An essential element of Christian fundamentalist belief is *dispensationalism*, a belief that God has divided history into different sections and rules differently in each one.[24] One of these sections, or stages, is the premillennial Second Coming of Jesus, or "rapture," when Jesus will "gather up the faithful" (and leave behind the unfaithful); this dispensation will be followed by the restoration of Israel and the return of Christ, who will rule for a thousand years (the "millennium"). Many "fantastic" apocalyptic events will occur at the end of time including the Battle of Armageddon, all chronicled in the Book of Revelation in the Christian Bible.

Similarly, Muslim fundamentalists have emphasized elements of belief and practice that offend the majority of Muslim believers in, from their point of view, their miraculous and extreme claims and acts. Muslim fundamentalists stress the Night Journey and Ascent of the Prophet as part of their sacred claim to Jerusalem. They have interpreted a particular Quranic verse (as have many Muslim Quranic commentaries) as indicating that Muhammad went in one night from Mecca to Jerusalem and back again on the back of a fabulous winged creature named Buraq. While in Jerusalem he led all the previous prophets (including Abraham, Moses, and Jesus) in prayer and then rose through the seven heavens and spoke to (though he did not see) God.[25] Sayyid Qutb, a well-known Egyptian fundamentalist, author of a famous Quranic commentary, and martyr of the fundamentalist cause in Egypt wrote an account of his contemporary Muslim society in Egypt in 1966 in which he described most Muslim Egyptians as living in the Age of Ignorance (*jahiliyya*). He suggested that they were like infidels because they were not practicing true Islam simply by observing regular prayer, fasting, and profession of faith. They needed to become militants to be true Muslims. This accusation outraged many Muslims in Egypt.[26]

Muslim fundamentalists have also emphasized certain radical punishments that have a Quranic basis and stipulated that "Islamic states" must enforce them, such as cutting off the right hand for theft and one hundred lashes of the whip for adultery.[27] Similarly there are certain radical dress codes having a Quranic basis,[28] establishing norms of modesty for women and men—but particularly for women such as veiling and covering the entire body including head, neck, and limbs—that fundamentalists enthusiastically seek to enforce where they have power and influence. Although veiling is generally perceived in the West as a traditional marker of Islamic culture, it has had a very recent resurgence connected to the resurgence of the fundamentalist movement. As a student in Cairo in 1955–1956 over a ten-month period and walking into every quarter of the central city, I never saw a veiled woman!

Describing the *haredim*, the ultraorthodox Jews of Israel, Heilman pointed to the "sweetness of extremism." By this term he wished to emphasize the fact that the *haredim* emphasize precisely those biblical customs that their opponents in the secular society reject.[29] Because contemporary Israeli society emphasizes the mixing of the sexes in public places, the *haredim* stress their separation. Because contemporary Israelis dress in bright colors, *haredim* insist on dressing in black and white. Because Hebrew is the official language of the state of Israel, they set themselves apart from it by speaking Yiddish.

In all these cases fundamentalists choose to emphasize precisely those elements in their scriptural tradition that will astonish, disturb, scandalize, and often outrage their secularized opponents. By and large western Christians are children of the Enlightenment, an intellectual movement that moved reason and science into first place. Christian fundamentalists, accordingly, emphasize the rising of the living from the dead, bodily ascension into heaven (against the laws of gravity), and the virgin birth in an age of sexual permissiveness. Fundamentalist Muslims emphasize the stipulated punishments of the Quran (*hudud*) not only because of their stern sense of justice for violations of the moral order, but because they know such stress will outrage their former colonial oppressors. And they emphasize veiling, in part, because they know it will offend western feminists whose values they repudiate, believing themselves in the complementarity of rights between men and women rather than in equality between them.

## Scripturalism and Militant Nationalism

"Nationalism, as a collective emotional force in our culture, makes its first appearance . . . in the Hebrew Bible."[30] The Irish scholar and statesman Donald C. O'Brien argues in his book *God Land: Reflections on Religion and Nationalism*, that in the first few books of the Bible, God chose a particular people and promised them a land. The Old Testament nationalist passages are powerful and the internationalist passages weak.

Another scholar, Naim S. Ateek, has identified three streams of tradition flowing from the Christian and Jewish scriptures: a Torah-oriented tradition, a Prophetic tradition, and a militant nationalist tradition.[31] The Torah-oriented tradition is oriented to the books of law (the Torah) and their observance as well as toward making peace with Hellenizers (the conquerors of the ancient Hebrews; i.e., the Greeks and Romans). This is the tradition that eventually produced the Talmud and the Mishnah, books of legal traditions and legal interpretations. The tradition was previously symbolized by the Pharisees. The Prophetic tradition emphasizes the universalistic character of God as the creator of the universe; emphasizes the land of Canaan as belonging to God, rather than the Israelites; and emphasizes that God is a god of justice who cares about the poor and the underprivileged. All claims on land are conditional on moral behavior. This tradition is associated with the prophets Isaiah, Jonah, and Amos; the disciples Matthew and Luke; and the Book of Acts.[32]

It is the third militant nationalist stream that is embraced by many Christian and Jewish fundamentalists. This stream is associated with the books of Joshua, 1 and 2 Judges, Samuel, 1 and 2 Kings, and Deuteronomy. Its heroes are the Maccabees and Zealots who resorted to armed insurrection and preferred death to surrender or accommodation to the Roman rulers. The third stream has direct social and military implications. The scriptures viewed with horror close social relations or intermarriage of the ancient Hebrews with other ethnic groups because it would destroy the purity of the seed of a covenanted people and endanger or defile their religion:

> You must not make a treaty with them or spare them. You must not intermarry with them, neither giving your daughters to their sons, nor taking their daughters for your sons; if you do, they will draw your sons away from the Lord and make them worship other gods. Then the Lord will be angry with you and will destroy you quickly. But this is what you must do to them; pull down their altars, break their sacred pillars, hack down their sacred poles and destroy their idols by fire, for you are a people holy to the Lord your God; the Lord your God chose you out of all nations on earth to be his special possession (Deuteronomy 7:1–6).[33]

Resorting to violence against the opponents of God's Chosen People and brutal retaliation for wrongs done is justified time and again in the scriptures:

> When the Lord your God brings you into the land which you are entering to occupy and drives out many nations before you—Hittites, Girgashites, Amorites, Canaanites, Perizzites, Hivites, and Jebusites, seven nations more numerous and powerful than you—when the Lord your God delivers them into your power and you defeat them, you must put them to death (Deuteronomy 7:1–2).

In one verse God commands Joshua, "you shall not leave any creature alive" (Deuteronomy 20:16–17). And scripture records Joshua's response:

> So Joshua massacred the population of the whole region—the hill-country, the Negeb, the Shephelah, the watersheds—and all their kings. He left not survivor, destroying everything that drew breath, as the Lord the God of Israel had commanded. Joshua carried the slaughter from Kadesh-barnea to Gaza, over the whole land of Goshen as far as Gibeon (Joshua 10:40–41).

And this commandment of violence had been based on an earlier one to Moses: "It was the Lord's purpose that they should offer an obstinate resistance to the Israelites in battle, and that thus they should be annihilated without mercy and utterly destroyed, as the Lord had commanded Moses" (Joshua 11:20).[34]

What were they fighting over and why was such violence ordained for the ancient Hebrews? They were fighting over a land, a holy land that had been covenanted to them by God, as recorded in the Bible several times. The first and territorially widest is the Abrahamic covenant appearing in Genesis 15:18–21:

> That very day the Lord made a covenant with Abraham and he said, "To your descendants I give this land from the River of Egypt [identified by the *Encyclopaedia Judaica* as the Nile River] to the Great River, the river Euphrates, the territory of the Kenites, Kenizzites, Kadomites, Hittites, Perizzites, Rephaim, Amorites, Canaanites, Girgash, Hivites and Jebusites."[35]

Other scriptural verses stipulate much narrower territorial ranges; for example, "from Dan to Beersheba" (2 Samuel 24:2 and 1 Kings 4:25) or more open-ended claims: "Every place where you set the soles of your feet shall be yours" (Deuteronomy 11:24).

Moreover, the militant nationalist scriptures in some places indicate that rights to the land are not based on moral rights or meritorious achievement but rather on God's (arbitrary) choice: "The Lord your God will bring you into the land which he swore to your forefathers Abraham, Isaac and Jacob that he would give you, a land of great and fine cities which you did not build, houses full of good things which you did not provide, rock-hewn cisterns which you did not hew, and vineyards and olive trees which you did not plant" (Deuteronomy 6:10).[36]

The justification of violence in the assertion of rights by a people to a holy land is also ingrained in the militant nationalist scriptures in the very role of God in the struggle of the ancient Hebrews to conquer and occupy their land. They had the conviction that God fought alongside his people. In the scriptures he is referred to as "the Lord of Hosts," a warrior who was accompanied by terrified natural phenomena on his marches: "Cloud-banks were before him, before him the clouds raced by Hail and coals of fire. He shot forth his arrows and scattered them, lightening bolts he flashed and put them in panic" (Psalm 18 [2 Samuel 22] 10ff).[37]

The reaction of nature to God's military onslaughts and his demeanor left no doubt about the legitimacy of the use of violence to defend the holy land:

> The earth quaked and shook; the foundations of the mountains shuddered; they quaked when the wrath waxed hot.
> Smoke arose from his nostrils, and fire devoured;
> Coals flamed forth from him. (Psalm 18:8ff)[38]

What is the connection of these verses of scripture addressed to the ancient Hebrews, to the contemporary political scene and fundamentalism? Historian Donald H. Akenson has made that connection clear. His book *God's Peoples* details how the peoples of three modern nations—South Africa, Ulster (Northern Ireland), and Israel—have taken scripture seriously, particularly that part of it that stipulates the Abrahamic, Mosaic, and Davidic covenants in which a people are "called by their God to wander the wilderness, defeat the heathen and to occupy a promised land."[39]

All three peoples celebrate a covenant, modeled on the biblical covenant, asserting the rights of a people to a modern nation-state. All three regard their land as holy, are profoundly attached to it, have undergone exodus (exile), and are righteous in their use of violence to gain it, hold it, and protect it.[40] For these fundamentalists, scripture is very much relevant to the modern world and the modern nation.

Finally, it must be emphasized that fundamentalists' relationship to scripture and their use of it is selective. This fact has been demonstrated repeatedly in this chapter. Fundamentalists select certain verses as proof-texts to support particular beliefs and legitimize particular practices. They select other verses particularly because they scandalize their opponents, and they select still others because they support their political claims to their national life in a certain nation-state.

## Notes

1. For instance, see Ammerman, *Bible Believers*; David O. Beale, *In Pursuit of Purity: American Fundamentalism since 1850* (Greenville, S.C.: Unusual Publications, 1986); Margaret Bendroth, *Fundamentalism and Gender, 1875 to the Present* (New Haven, Conn.: Yale University Press, 1993); Kepel, *The Revenge of God*; Lustick, *For the Land and the Lord*; Martin Marty and Scott Appleby, *Fundamentalisms Observed* (Chicago: University of Chicago Press, 1991) and *The Glory and the Power: The Fundamentalist Challenge to the Modern World* (Boston: Beacon Press, 1992); Munson, *The House of Si Abd Allah* and *Religion and Power in Morocco*; and Alan Peshkin, *God's Choice: The Total World of a Fundamentalist Christian School* (Chicago: University of Chicago Press, 1986).

2. In a debate on the inerrancy of the Bible between two notable Christian preachers in 1923, the fundamentalist preacher in the debate admitted the necessity of interpretation of the sacred text by the use of both contextual reasoning and metaphorical reading and admitted as well the presence of contradictions in the sacred text as follows: "So, if we had a full understanding of all the conditions of life and the circumstances under which the several narratives in the Bible were recorded, we would doubtless find that many of these difficulties [i.e., contradictions] would disappear."

And again interpretation in reference to the biblical reference to the numbers of legs of certain insects being four:

the Bible in connection with grasshoppers, locusts, and crickets, which are spoken of as going on all fours, when they have six legs. But while it is true that the Palestinian locust has six legs, it walks on only four forward legs.

It is well known that the ancient Hebrews spoke of any animal that did not walk upright as "going on all fours."

And metaphorical interpretation of the biblical reference to the sun standing still: "Who would say it was untrue if I declared that 'I saw a beautiful sunrise this morning.' Now I really saw no such thing. What I actually saw was an earth-roll, not a sun-rise. The sun doesn't 'rise,' yet we so say."

See also "The Debates between John Roach Straton and Charles Francis Potter," in *Fundamentalist vs. Modernist*, ed. Joel A. Carpenter (New York: Garland Publishing Company, 1988), 71–73 for details.

3. Munson, *The House of Si Abd Allah*, 183.

4. Munson *The House of Si Abd Allah*, 182–83.

5. As quoted in Karen Armstrong, *The Battle for God* (New York: Alfred A. Knopf, 2000), 40.

6. Armstrong, *The Battle for God*, 39.

7. Carpenter, *Fundamentalist vs. Modernist*, 43.

8. As quoted in Antoun, *Muslim Preacher in the Modern World*, 260.

9. As quoted in Munson, *The House of Si Abd Allah*, 67–68.

10. Munson, *The House of Si Abd Allah*, 63.

11. As quoted in Peshkin, *God's Choice*, 258.

12. Peshkin, *God's Choice*, 258.

13. *The Bible: Revised Standard Edition*, 1952, New Testament, John 14:6.

14. Carpenter, *Fundamentalist vs. Modernist*, 38.

15. Carpenter, *Fundamentalist vs. Modernist*, 46.

16. For detailed accounts of the rise of religious movements, events leading up to the Iranian revolution, the religious culture of Iran, and the symbolic significance of Khomeini's victory, see Michael Fischer, *Iran*; and Ervand Abrahamian, *Khomeinism: Essays on the Islamic Republic* (Berkeley: University of California Press, 1993).

17. Iranian Shi'ites compose a major sect in Islam. Although they follow the five pillars of Islam (prayer, fasting, pilgrimage to Mecca, alms-giving, and profession of faith) with all other Muslims, they are distinctive in many aspects of ritual and in the emotional tenor of their faith.

18. As quoted in *New York Times*, 1 November 1979.

19. See Luther Gerlach and Virginia Hine, *People, Power, Change: Movements of Social Transformation* (Indianapolis: Bobbs Merrill, 1970), chapter six for details of the argument.

20. As quoted in *New York Times*, 15 June 1987.

21. As quoted in Marty and Appleby, *The Glory and the Power*, 22.

22. See Marty and Appleby, *The Glory and the Power*, 63, for details.

23. Peter Montagnon, *Protestant Spirit U.S.A.* (London: The BBC, 1977), film.

24. See Marty and Appleby, *The Glory and the Power*, 50–51, for details.

25. See the account of Muhammad's Night Journey and Ascent by Imam Najm ad-Din al-Ghaiti in Arthur Jeffrey, *A Reader on Islam: Passages from Standard Arabic Writings Illustrative of the Beliefs and Practices of Muslims* ('s-Gravenhage: Mouton, 1962).

26. The book is entitled *Milestones*. See Gilles Kepel, *Muslim Extremism in Egypt: The Prophet and the Pharoh* (Berkely: University of California, 1986) and Ibrahim M. Abu-Rabi', *Intellectual Origins of Islamic Resurgence in the Muslim Arab World*, (Albany: State University of New York Press, 1996) chapter six for details.

27. Most interpretations of Islamic law, however, lay down very elaborate rules of evidence for proving theft or adultery in an Islamic court, and as a result the penalties are seldom carried out even in Islamic states enforcing Islamic law. On the rules of evidence for proving theft, see David F. Forte, "Islamic Law and the Crime of Theft: An Introduction," *Cleveland State Law Review* 34, no. 1, 1985–86.

28. However, many of the verses of the Quran urging modest dress for women are addressed to the Prophet's wives and not to the generality of women, and Muslims are divided on the circumstances requiring the enforcement of modesty norms. For a detailed analysis of the significance of the code of modesty for Muslim women in Muslim Arab villages and particularly in rural Jordan in the 1960s including the Quranic basis for such norms, see Richard Antoun, "On the Modesty of Women in Arab Muslim Villages: A Study in the Accommodation of Traditions," *American Anthropologist* 70, no. 4 (August 1968).

29. See Heilman, *Defenders of the Faith*, 138.

30. As quoted by Conor Cruise O'Brien in *God Land: Reflections on Religion and Nationalism* (Cambridge, Mass.: Harvard University Press, 1988), 2.

31. See Naim S. Ateek, *Justice, and Only Justice: A Palestinian Theology of Liberation* (Maryknoll, N.Y.: Orbis Books, 1989) for details of the argument.

32. See Ateek, chapter four for details.

33. See Bashir K. Nijim, "Biblical Zionism and Political Zionism," in *American Church Politics and the Middle East*, ed. B. K. Nijim (Belmont, Mass.: Association of American-Arab University Graduates, 1982) for a discussion of the implications of this and the following verses. Not all books of the Hebrew Bible

stipulate an exclusive militant nationalist perspective. For instance, in the Book of Ruth, Ruth (a Moabite) followed her Jewish husband in an interethnic marriage that was perfectly acceptable. Fundamentalists do not refer to such examples from scripture.

34. As quoted in Nijim, "Biblical Zionism and Political Zionism," 31.

35. As quoted in Nijim, "Biblical Zionism and Political Zionism," 22.

36. See Hassan S. Haddad in *American Church Politics and the Middle East*, 15 for details.

37. As quoted in Leonard Greenspoon, "The Warrior God or God, the Divine Warrior," in *Religion and Politics in the Modern World*, ed. Peter H. Merkl and Ninian Smart (New York: New York University Press, 1983).

38. As quoted in Greenspoon, 213. See his interesting discussion of the relationship between the scriptures and the military ethos of the ancient Hebrews.

39. As quoted in Donald H. Akenson, *God's Peoples: Covenant and Land in South Africa, Israel and Ulster* (Ithaca, N.Y.: Cornell University Press, 1992), 4.

40. See Akenson, *God's Peoples*, parts one and two for the argument.

# THE PAST IN THE PRESENT: "TRADITIONING," THE PROOF-TEXT, AND THE COVENANT

Samuel Heilman has defined the process of "traditioning" as "the need to demonstrate that there is nothing so ancient and archaic in the Jewish past that it does not have its place in the Jewish present."[1] For the *haredim* "the Bible was not just an account of the dawn of Israelite peoplehood but a code book for Jewish behavior. The lives of its heroes were not simply the stuff of stories but archetypes for contemporary behavior."[2] "In short, there was nothing so old that it was meaningless."[3]

The process of blurring "now" with the "mythic past" is not confined to the *haredim* but is generally characteristic of Christian and Muslim fundamentalists as well.[4] In this chapter we will examine the *haredi* case, a Muslim Jordanian case, and an American Christian case, then analyze the biblical covenant as an example of traditioning in the modern state of South Africa.

An underlying factor in claiming the immediate relevance of the distant past for the present is the quest for authenticity. Whereas the historic circumstances for the yearning for authenticity differ with the three religious traditions—the Holocaust for Jews, colonialism for Middle Eastern Muslims, and the spread of science (as seen in the doctrines of evolution and the higher criticism) and mass migration for American Christians—the quest is the same. Fundamentalists in all three faiths seek to sharply distinguish themselves from the surrounding majoritarian secular society and authenticate themselves in terms of a hallowed past, whether by dress, by demeanor, by food, by sleep, by worship (modes of prayer, fasting, pilgrimage), by language, by law, or by labeling (self-identity).

Another factor underlying the fundamentalists penchant to engage in traditioning is their belief in the struggle between good and evil. The authenticated beliefs, styles, and actions represent the power of good and their opposite represent the power of evil. Fundamentalists define themselves in large part by what they are *against*. They always have a very real and easily identifiable enemy. Quite often there are two enemies, the external enemy and the internal enemy, and frequently more animosity is reserved for the internal than the external enemy. For the *haredim* the external enemy are the goyim (gentiles) and the *chutz la'aretz*, those "outside the land (of Israel)," (particularly represented by the Arabs and often labeled Amelekites) the biblical people who symbolized evil for the ancient Hebrews.[5] The internal enemy are the secularized Jews, *chiloinim* (who form the majority in Israel), often called *maskilim*, literally "those who ask questions" (i.e., of scripture). They are viewed as doubters of God's words and underminers of faith.[6]

For many American Christian fundamentalists, the external enemy is the denier of God's words—particularly the communist, the atheist, and the secular humanist—and often members of other faiths. The internal and more dangerous enemies are the nonfundamentalist Christians who claim to be followers of Jesus but accept the norms laid down by the state and other nonreligious institutions in their daily lives and cavort with members of the secular society (e.g., the National Council of Churches). For fundamentalist Muslims in Egypt the external enemies are the colonialists and postcolonialists (including the Zionists), and the internal enemies are the *jahili* (hypocritical) Muslims who acquiesce to state edicts and secular norms while pretending to be Muslims by fasting and performing daily prayers (see chapter four).

The process of traditioning, then, is the process of identifying with the good past at the same time that it is the process of melding that past with the good present. The collapsing of the past and the present is clear in the *haredi* use of language. Heilman observed a *haredi* teacher quote a biblical commentary in Hebrew (which the students understood), and after each quote, translate it into Yiddish. Often he would follow a reference to Israel with the word *Yidn*, the Yiddish word for Jews (i.e., the authentic Jews).[7] Why did he do this? He did it to emphasize the authentic past of the *haredim*, the past of eastern Europe from whence their ancestors, particularly their religious leaders, came early in the century. He also did it to contrast that past to the modern present of Israeli society whose official modern language is Hebrew as well as with the ancient Hebrew past whose subject was the commentaries.[8]

The process of traditioning becomes clearer in Heilman's account of the sixth grade *haredi* students' knowledge of modern geography. Heilman asked the students to draw a map of (modern) Israel. They could not (they had never seen such a map). No one could list the names of the countries surrounding Israel nor name the main bodies of water, the Dead Sea and the Sea of Galilee. They had never heard of Saudi Arabia.[9] But they did have a map of the world. It was depicted on a globe hanging from the vestibule of the yeshiva (Jewish religious school). It was a map of eastern Europe that spread-eagled the globe. However, it was a very particular Eastern eastern Europe, the eastern Europe of the rebbes (Jewish scholar–mystics) who had founded the religious order in Russia and Poland more than a century before. The central focus of the map was the town of Zvil (the rebbe of the Israeli order to which the school was affiliated traced his descent to Zvil), and the surrounding cities were all well-known centers of authentic Jewish life in eastern Europe a hundred years previously. The past was made present in the geography taught as well as the language (Yiddish). Of course, the students had an excellent knowledge of scriptural geography, the geography of the Torah. For these yeshiva students, the Israel of their imagination, biblical Israel— including all its heroes and heroines—was far superior to modern (secularized) Israel, which in a sense represented the internal enemy.[10]

The past was made present in many other aspects of *haredi* life. For instance, Heilman attended the Friday night Sabbath religious observances at the "Belz" (an east European town) yeshiva in Jerusalem, which was culminated by a meal at the rebbe's *tish* (the Yiddish world for table). He described it as a "classic east European Jewish meal" that became ritualized.[11] After each set of songs, all Belz tunes, the rebbe ate another course, beginning with the breaking of coiled challah bread and followed in turn by gefilte fish, grape juice, chicken soup, farfel (little bits of noodles), honey-sweetened carrots, chicken, and finally fruit compote.

The *haredi* way of dealing with the tragedy of the Holocaust was to intensify both worship and what they regarded as the pure Jewish tradition (of eastern Europe) in all its aspects, and to nurture a counterculture through social separation (see chapter four).

One more example of traditioning involving scripture illustrates the point that for the fundamentalist, "life as perceived in sacred texts and life as it is lived are presumed interchangeable."[12] One day the teacher suddenly posed the question to the students in the kindergarten, "What is *ma'aser* (tithing)?" and followed it by another, "And to whom do we give it?"[13] The Bible has detailed prescriptions on tithing. Many children answered from the ancient Hebrew context, "to the priest, to the Levite (an ancient ritual sacrifice specialist), and to the poor." But the teacher, Yitzak, did not allow the answers in the ancient context to stand:

> He pointed to a drawing on the wall of a produce market like the one in the neighborhood outside the schoolroom. In the picture boys could see a greengrocer handing over some fruits and vegetables to a bearded *haredi*. "He's collecting *ma'aser*," Yitzak explained. To the boys who passed the vegetable stalls on their way to or from school, the scene was familiar. In many stores and stalls they could see signs that said TITHES HAVE BEEN TAKEN. They had learned to buy only from a grocer who gave *ma'aser*.[14]

## Parties (*Ahzab*) and Traditioning

Now let us cross the Jordan River and examine traditioning in the Jordanian Muslim village in which I have conducted anthropological research during the last forty years. Very early in my stay there I was warned not to visit the house of a man (I was conducting a household census of every village family) who was living by himself and raising hundreds of chickens. Aside from the fact that he was in his late thirties and unmarried and that he was raising chickens scientifically for profit (rather than for subsistence as others did), I was warned off him because he was a *hizbi*.

*Hizb* is the term of reference for a modern "political party" in the Arab world. In its adjectival form, *hizbi*, it meant "partyman." I discovered that this man, a native villager, had been arrested for distributing literature for a Muslim political party in town. At that time (the 1960s), political parties and political party activity were prohibited in Jordan. After serving a term in prison he had been released on condition that he remain in his native village and its environs; that is, he had been banished to the area. That is when he decided to raise chickens. But he continued to be known as a *hizbi*, a man associated with a political party (any political party), which was clearly a pejorative term for all villagers.

Because I had cultivated the friendship of the village preacher, read the Quran with him, and regularly attended his sermons, I also read the terms *hizb*, *ahzab* (plural form), and *hizbiyun* (party devotees) in the Quran, and heard the preacher use them in sermons, almost always in a pejorative sense. Although the Quran refers to "God's party" (*hizballah*), whose members are rewarded in the hereafter,[15] it has many more references to Satan's party: "Satan has gained mastery over them, and caused them to forget God's Remembrance. Those are Satan's party (*hizb*); why, Satan's party, surely they are the losers!" (58:19)[16]

Even when the Quranic reference is not to Satan, the reference to party or parties is overwhelmingly negative:

> But the parties (*ahzab*) have fallen into variance among themselves (19:37).
>
> And those to whom we have given the Book rejoice in what is sent down unto thee; and of the parties (*ahzab*) some reject some of it. Say: "I have only been commanded to serve God, and not to associate aught with Him. To Him I call and to Him I turn (13:36).
>
> And what of him who stands upon a clear sign from his Lord, and a witness from Him recites it, and before him the Book of Moses for an example and a mercy? Those believe in it; but whosoever disbelieves in it, being one of the partisans (*ahzab*) his promised land is the Fire (11:17)
>
> Messengers, eat of the good things and do righteousness; surely I know the things you do. Surely this community of yours is one community, and I am your Lord; so fear Me. But they split in their affair between them into sects, each party (*hizb*) rejoicing in what is with them. So leave them in their perplexity for a time (23:51–54).[17]

The negative references in these Quranic verses are clear: parties are those who spread error, ignore the call of God's prophets, sow social dissension, and factionalize into sects even when they are members of the same religion. Party activity is largely the struggle of evil forces against the good.

In the modern world political parties (also termed *ahzab*) have nothing to do with the biblical or Quranic prophets; they are not countergroups who repudiate prophetic messages and they are not religious sects. But the village preacher made his attitude toward modern political parties quite clear to me on more than one occasion: "The National Syrian Party, the Resurrection Party, the National Socialist Party, the Communist Party—they're all the same, communist."[18] When I asked the preacher why these parties were so popular he replied:

> Colonialism—it was what gave birth to the parties. There is a saying, "Divide and rule." The English are the origin of the [modern] parties. This happened in the time of the English; the father was for a party, the son was for (another) party, and the daughter was for (another) party; and when they sat down at the table together to eat, they fought with one another.[19]

The preacher went on to describe the local school scene in the 1950s before parties were banned:

> [During the party period] there were many political parties in Deir Abu Said [where the junior high school was located]. Teachers were not on speaking terms with one another and each had their own coterie of students who were always quarreling on the playground; and education went by the boards. Teachers went around flunking students not of their party.[20]

These attitudes toward political party activity and elections contested by political parties are widely shared among villagers who believe strongly in an ethos of consensus and reconciliation; "party" activity for them "disturbs the educational process . . . breaks up kinship ties including the ties of the nuclear family; . . . confounds religion; and . . . undermines the process of consensus by which social harmony is achieved in the community."[21]

The preacher united the Quranic view of party devotees (*hizbiyyun*) "as hypocrites, agents of the devil, repudiators of the prophets, spreaders of

error, and agents of schism with the modern evaluation of political parties as destroyers of family lines, underminers of family discipline, sowers
of community dissension, and demeanors of individual honor."[22] From
this Muslim village perspective, political activity does not require political parties, or if it does, only one party—the "party of God."

The melding of the Quranic meaning of *hizb* and the modern meaning
of *hizb* is an excellent example of the process of traditioning, making the
past part of the present. In the 1960s Jordanian peasants evaluated political party activity negatively, and in this evaluation they did not distinguish between *hizb* as God's party or Satan's party and *hizb* as modern political party. "*Hizb*, as defined by the preacher and interpreted by the
peasants, is a multivocal symbol [with many meanings] in which the
Quranic transcendental and social . . . implications of the term are inter-
woven with its modern nationalist and colonialist implications."[23] The
parties of the prophets' times (including Moses, Muhammad, and Jesus)[24]
and the parties of the modern state of Jordan had direct implications for
one another. Indeed, in the imaginations of villagers these parties were
the same. Their attributes were the same and their ethical implications
for Muslims were the same: the necessity of Muslims to struggle against
parties or factions that broke up the unity of the divine message (scriptures) and disturbed social harmony by sowing seeds of dissension.

## Traditioning in the United States

The Bethany Baptist Academy (BBA) provides an excellent example of
traditioning in the United States. Traditioning at BBA is focused on the
use of proof-texts that provide the fixed standards and final authority for
certain beliefs and practices. At the academy "educators . . . edify, cajole,
and threaten them [students] to be immersed in the Word [scriptures],
and to obey and to promulgate what they've heard."[25] Peshkin emphasizes
the omnipresence of the biblical text and the living relevance of particular scriptural verses to the teachers' and students' daily lives: "It is the
words. They roll about, pouring forth anywhere at any time, shalts and
shalt nots piling up, a scriptural pearl never more than a breath away."[26]

Teachers at BBA regard obedience to parents and teachers as a critical matter and they constantly cite biblical verses that emphasize obedience: "Obey them that rule over you, and submit your selves" (Hebrews 3:17); "Children obey your parents in the Lord" (Ephesians 6:1); "Behold, to obey is better than sacrifice" [sacrifice was a primary ritual obligation for the ancient Hebrews] (1 Samuel 15:22);[27] "rebellion is as the sin of witch-craft" (1 Samuel 15:23);[28] and "Whosoever be that doth rebel against thy commandment he shall be put to death" (Joshua 1:18).[29]

One of the teachers at BBA indicated how the verses on obedience personally affected her when she was a young girl. She had been dating an unsaved boy strongly disapproved by her parents. Scriptural prohibitions against socializing with "non-Christians," including from the fundamentalist perspective the unsaved, are quite specific: "Be ye not unequally yoked with unbelievers" (2 Corinthians 6:14).[30] So in dating this boy she had contravened two scriptural norms, one on obedience and another on socializing. One day she reversed herself: "It just hit me that if I didn't do what the Lord wanted me to do, I really don't think I'd be here now. I think he would have said, 'Girl, I don't know how much more I can take.' I always had a fear of the Lord, and then it dawned on me, 'Wow, I don't want to die.'"[31]

Teachers who were concerned about exuberant excesses of students such as chewing gum, listening to hard rock, dancing, kissing, drinking, smoking, and going to parties cited 2 Timothy 2:22: "So shun youthful passions and aim at righteousness, faith, love and peace along with those who call upon the Lord from a pure heart."

Students who wished to help their deviant friends reform cited biblical verses to one another, for as one said, "your friends won't listen to you if you just say they're wrong."[32] Just as their own parents matched advice with a biblical proof-text, they did the same with their friends.

For instance, one student was concerned about another schoolmate who was constantly venting her anger because the gym instructor always yelled at her for being slow about putting on her gym clothes. She acted accordingly: "So I took God's word and showed how she shouldn't get mad, but she should try harder to please God and Miss Bennett [the teacher]."[33]

Sometimes the students and teacher hear scriptural themes at one or two removes from the text but continue to act on them in their daily lives. One young teacher had been reluctant to accede to the urgings of others to give talks at other churches because she felt lacking in biblical learning. One day she heard a moving song on the radio, "The King Is Coming," about the Second Coming of Christ: "I got so thrilled thinking about this that I felt the Lord had just spoke to me. He wanted me to speak publicly, laid it out upon my heart. Right out loud I said, "OK, Lord, if you want me to speak publicly, I will."[34]

Traditioning also occurs in the field of sex roles and social relations within the family. Fundamentalists at BBA strongly believe in the sexual division of labor, with sons learning "craft skills, work habits, gardening, manners, economics, leadership, music and rhetoric" while daughters needed to learn "cooking, housekeeping, household management, manners, sewing, growing and arranging flowers, interior decoration, literary skills, and child care."[35] The culminating proof-text that is always cited to affirm the self-evident patripotestal (power of the father) character of the marital relationship is Ephesians 5:21–22.

> Be subject to one another out of reverence for Christ. Wives be subject to your husbands, as to the Lord. For the husband is the head of the wife as Christ is head of the church, his body, and is himself its Saviour. As the church is subject to Christ, so let wives be subject in everything to their husbands.[36]

The use of proof-texts to introduce the past into the present is not limited to ethics, as all the examples above indicated. Proof-texts are also used to affirm and legitimate key articles of faith such as the belief that Jesus saves (i.e., grants salvation to all true believers):

> But God shows his love for us in that while we were yet sinners Christ died for us. Since, therefore, we are now justified by his blood, much more shall we be saved by him from the wrath of God (Romans 5:8–9).[37]
>
> Because if you confess with your lips that Jesus is Lord and believe in your heart that God raised him from the dead, you will be saved (Romans 10:9).[38]
>
> For the wages of sin is death, but the free gift of God is eternal life in Christ Jesus our Lord (Romans 6:23).[39]

At the BBA, the citation of proof-texts on an everyday basis to affirm ethics and belief by teachers, students, principal, and parents is a constant and active form of traditioning.

## Traditioning and the Covenant in South Africa

The last chapter suggested that the biblical covenant formed the ideological basis for modern forms of militant nationalism. "The Covenant" and the affiliated ideas of the promised land, the exile (exodus), and the sacrifice also dramatically illustrate the pertinence of the process of traditioning for the foundation of modern nation-states. This illustration will be drawn out in detail for the case of South Africa.[40] The descendants of Dutch, German, and French settlers in South Africa developed a framework for a modern nation in the nineteenth century based on the formulation, application, and celebration of particular biblical concepts and events. First, we will outline these biblical concepts and events and then we will trace their application to the modern South African case.

The historian Akenson has argued that certain South Africans (early on called Boers but later termed Afrikaners, after their formalization of the Afrikaans language as one of the official languages of South Africa)[41] read the Christian scriptures as manuals of instruction for modern society and modern politics, determining "what people would believe . . . think . . . and . . . do."[42] The Afrikaners drew selectively on the first five books of the Bible and focused on the idea of a covenant with God, first spoken to Abraham:

> And I will make of thee a great nation, and I will bless thee, and make thy name great, and thou shalt be a blessing: And I will bless them that bless thee, and curse them that curse thee: and in thee shall be all the families of the earth be blessed (Gen. 12:2–3).[43]
>
> And I will make thee exceedingly fruitful, and I will make nations of thee, and kings shall come out of thee. And I will establish my covenant between me and thee and thy seed after thee in generations for an everlasting covenant, to be a God unto thee, and to thy seed after thee. And I will give unto thee, and to thy seed after thee, the land wherein thou art a stranger, all the land of Canaan, for an everlasting possession; and I will be their God (Gen. 17:6–8).[44]

This biblical covenant is conditional on Abraham's leaving his father and relatives and following God to a land still undisclosed, and also on his being circumcised.

Later God covenants with Moses and his people to lead the ancient Hebrews out of Egypt, but again on the condition that they obey the ten commandments as well as "a complex set of rules" set down in the books Exodus and Deuteronomy.[45] Moreover, the ancient Hebrews were called on by their God to undergo exile, wandering, and numerous trials and tribulations; that is, to sacrifice for their religion. The biblical covenant, then, sets up a three-way relationship between God, a people, and a land—the land here being geographically specific and demarcated in the scriptures.[46]

This relationship is conditional, perpetual, and unfolding. That is, each later episode of contractual relations builds on and informs an earlier episode. In the first five books of the Bible the ancient Hebrews are regarded as a chosen people with a "corporate personality" (i.e., a people who are treated as one for the purpose of the contract, and, moreover, a people who extend into the past and the future in perpetuity).[47] They are held to account, rewarded, and punished as a single entity.

Akenson has underlined that the habit of mind associated with the biblical covenant divides the world into the pure (sacred) and the impure (profane): "But I have said unto you, ye shall inherit their land, and I will give it unto you to possess it, a land that floweth with milk and honey: I *am* the Lord your God, which have separated you from *other* people. . . . And ye shall be holy unto me: for I, the Lord, *am* holy, and have severed you from *other* people, that ye should be mine" (Lev. 20:24–26).[48]

Therefore, the ancient Hebrews were continually concerned with issues of purity and separation, having to discern whether every stranger was one of them.

The Afrikaners in South Africa also underwent exodus and exile, endured blood sacrifices, and developed a national consciousness as a unitary people in the process of bringing the scripture to life in their own circumstances, and by covenanting and recovenanting with God for a specific promised land.

From 1806 to 1948 the Afrikaners were under alien rule, dominated by an Anglo-Celtic culture very different than their own and by the political control of the British Empire. As English settlers came into South Africa and the British imperial government began a policy of anglicization in South Africa—reserving government positions for English speakers and requiring all official documents to be in English (although the great majority of the people were not English)—Afrikaners reacted in 1836 by beginning the "Great Trek" from the Cape Province in the southwest of the country to the Transvaal in the northeast, a distance of 1,000 miles by foot and ox-wagon.[49]

This exodus and exile for the purpose of escaping English influence and preserving what they regarded as the purity of their culture and their race began a long period of what they interpreted as God-ordained tribulation. In their new territory they were ambushed by the Zulu in 1838, and on December 16 of that year fought 10,000 Zulu warriors in the Battle of Blood River. Three thousand Zulu were killed (by firearms) without any Afrikaner fatalities, a victory that they celebrated as ordained by God.

In 1852 and 1853 the British imperial government recognized the independence of two Afrikaner states, the Transvaal and the Orange Free State. But with the discovery of diamonds in Afrikaner country in 1867, the imperial government quickly moved to establish military control in the Transvaal and the Orange Free State, canceling the Great Trek's aim of liberation from alien rule. The Afrikaners rebelled and fought two successive "Anglo-Boer Wars" (1880–1881 and 1899–1902), which resulted in a decisive British victory and much suffering for the Afrikaners.

However, Akenson points out that instead of resulting in the crushing of Afrikaner nationalism and the aspiration for an Afrikaner state, the decisive defeat of the Afrikaners at the hands of the most powerful empire of the day solidified their sense of unitary peoplehood and intensified their drive for cultural separation.[50] How can one explain this counterintuitive result? In great part by the process of traditioning by which the biblical covenant was repeatedly integrated into the theology and politics of South African life. On December 16, 1938, 100,000 people attended a ceremony in Pretoria, the capital of South Africa, to commemorate the victory of the Afrikaners' forbears over the Zulu one hundred years before at Blood River. The number in attendance composed one-tenth of the total Afrikaner population in the Union of South Africa.[51] Many Afrikaner men affirmed their ethnic identity by growing beards and women wore costumes like those worn by women on the Great Trek a century before. Many Afrikaners simulated the Great Trek and converged on Blood River in ox-wagons after passing many small towns in the South African countryside.[52]

During these ceremonies that were held at Capetown and Blood River as well as at Pretoria, the Afrikaner Covenantal Oath, said to have been repeated by many Afrikaner fighters on the eve of their battle with the Zulu a century before, was repeated by the assembled:

> My brethren and fellow countrymen, at this moment we stand before the holy God of heaven and earth, to make a promise, if He will be with us and protect us and deliver the enemy into our hands so that we may triumph over him, that we shall observe the day and the date as an anniversary in each year and a day of thanksgiving like the Sabbath, in His honour; and that we shall enjoin our children that they must take part with us in this, for a remembrance even for our posterity; and if anyone sees a difficulty in this, let him return from this place. For the honour of His name shall be joyfully exalted, and to Him the fame and the honour of the victory must be given.[53]

After 1938 the "Day of the Covenant" was commemorated nationally on an annual basis. In 1980 it became the "Day of the Vow."

In 1880 to commemorate their successful fighting in the first Boer War, Afrikaner men in the Transvaal had come together and built a stone altar "as a sign of their covenant with each other and with Yahweh."[54] And on Covenant Day 1891 Paul Kruger, the president of the Transvaal, drew parallels with an earlier covenant when he said: "It is for God that we have prepared the feast in His honour. . . . In the Old Testament, God said to Abraham: "The covenant which I made with you and your descendants, excluding none, shall remain before you and your seed from now to eternity."[55]

In 1895 the clergyman who delivered the main address on the Day of the Covenant used as his text this biblical verse: "But my servant Caleb, because he had another spirit with him, and hath followed me fully, him I will bring into the land whereinto he went; and his seed shall possess it" (Num. 14:24).[56]

It is clear that Afrikaner statesmen, clergymen, and laymen (over a time that hearkened back to the past and looked into the future) conceived of their relationship to God as one entirely personal but also entirely collective—with a people as a single entity. They brought forth scripture as a living demonstration of their right to a particular land, a mandate to conquer it, and a legitimation of social legislation to enshrine separation and purification of the people and the culture.

There followed in the twentieth century numerous pieces of legislation (e.g., 1913 Land Act, 1923 Natives [Urban Areas] Act, 1926 Colour Bar Act) that reserved lands and jobs for white Afrikaners.[57] Laws of color segregation and prohibition of miscegenation were also rooted in scriptural imperatives (e.g., those accounts of Ham's [Ham symbolizing the nonwhite races] committing a sin against the seed and against the purity of the chosen people by looking at his father Noah's nakedness). Ham's descendants were cursed and were ordained to be the servants of the chosen people thereafter. A biblical account relating to the ancient Canaanites, then, was made immediately relevant to the South African context and applied to nonwhites in relation to their Afrikaner lords.[58]

To return to our earlier question: How is it that after undergoing exile, defeat in two wars, displacement into concentration camps, and continued harassment and discrimination by the most powerful imperial system in the world, the Afrikaners not only survived but also (after 125 years) went on to claim victory in a nation-state where they were a minority? The answer is that they were inspired by a religious imagination conceived in terms of a set of powerful metaphors: an ancient covenant, a chosen people, a blessed land, a sacrifice in exodus and exile, and a purification of the land through conquest and through separation from the impure (peoples and cultures). They were able to interpret these theological metaphors in such a way as to explain their own past suffering, their present victories and defeats, and their auspicious future as inheritors of a sacred land. The Bible is a living document for them, explaining defeats in terms of the immorality of the people and victories as rewards of a living God for their faith and pure practice.[59] The existence of the Afrikaner nation-state and its accompanying ideology after over a century of struggle is an important example of the process of traditioning on the grand political and social scale.

# Notes

1. Heilman, *Defenders of the Faith*, 203.
2. Heilman, *Defenders of the Faith*, 204.
3. Ibid.
4. I am adopting the anthropological usage of "myth" here. That usage puts aside the question of historical truth. Rather, a myth is a story believed by the people. It may be "true" or "untrue" in the sense of being historically verifiable. What matters is that it is believed in and acted on.
5. See Heilman, *Defenders of the Faith*, 232–33 ff. for details.
6. See Heilman, *Defenders of the Faith*, 146–47 for details.
7. See Heilman, *Defenders of the Faith*, 195 and 248 for details.
8. That the *haredim* identify with a past and speak a language that is different than the majority of Jews in Israel who identify with the modern Zionist secular state of Israel is not new in its inspiration. As Juergensmeyer (*The New Cold War?*, 63) has noted, "Tensions between the religious and secular dimensions of modern Israel have existed throughout the almost 100-year history of the movement for nationhood." When Theodore Herzl founded the World Zionist Organization in 1897, aiming to found a modern state with "a new, modern symbol system—a state, a social order of their own, above all a flag," religious nationalists immediately dissented and founded their own organizations. They founded Mizrahi, which aimed at the formation of a religious state based on the Torah, and Agudat Israel, which supported settling Jews in Palestine but refused to give allegiance to any Jewish state established by human beings, claiming there could be no true Israel "until the temple was rebuilt and a new David was installed as king." See Juergensmeyer (*The New Cold War?*, 63–64 ff.) for details. Thus although for most Jews the state of Israel that was founded in 1948 was the desired religious or cultural society, for Jewish fundamentalists it was a secular state that followed the rules of Euro-American society and would only result in the assimilation of Jews and the loss of any genuine religious society.
9. See Heilman, *Defenders of the Faith*, 233–34.
10. Heilman, *Defenders of the Faith*, 234.
11. Heilman, *Defenders of the Faith*, 89.
12. Heilman, *Defenders of the Faith*, 188. Here, Heilman's *haredi* example is applicable in its general significance for fundamentalists of other religions.
13. Heilman, *Defenders of the Faith*, 204.
14. Ibid.
15. See Quran, 5:56 and 58:22.

16. As quoted in Antoun, *Muslim Preacher in the Modern World*, 92.

17. All these verses are as quoted in Antoun, *Muslim Preacher in the Modern World*, 93–94.

17. As quoted in Antoun, *Muslim Preacher in the Modern World*, 204.

19. Ibid.

20. Ibid.

21. As quoted in Antoun, *Muslim Preacher in the Modern World*, 207.

22. Ibid.

23. As quoted in Antoun, *Muslim Preacher in the Modern World*, 211–212.

24. From the Muslim perspective, Moses, Muhammad, and Jesus were all prophets and messengers (receivers of a sacred scripture who transmitted it to a people), and they were all opposed by "parties" (i.e., factions that arose to oppose them and the message [scripture] they delivered).

25. As quoted in Peshkin, *God's Choice*, 113.

26. Ibid.

27. As quoted in *The Bible*, 1 Samuel 15:22, Revised Standard Edition (London: Collins, 1952).

28. As quoted in Peshkin, *God's Choice*, 43.

29. Ibid.

30. As quoted in Peshkin, *God's Choice*, 128.

31. As quoted in Peshkin, *God's Choice*, 44.

32. Peshkin, *God's Choice*, 162.

33. Ibid.

34. Peshkin, *God's Choice*, 45.

35. Peshkin, *God's Choice*, 127.

36. As quoted in *The Bible*, Ephesians 5: 21-22, Revised Standard Edition (London: Collins, 1946).

37. *The Bible*, Romans 5:8–9.

38. *The Bible*, Romans 10:9.

39. *The Bible*, Romans 6:23.

40. It could have been drawn out for the cases of modern Israel and Ulster (Northern Ireland). See Akenson, *God's Peoples*, for details.

41. Afrikaans was the common language spoken by the Dutch, German, and French settlers in South Africa in the nineteenth century. It was a kind of rural dialect and not written to any extent until the end of the nineteenth century. The Afrikaner national resurgence at the beginning of the twentieth century resulted in a florescence of literature in Afrikaans and the formal acceptance of Afrikaans as an official language of South Africa (along with English) in 1925.

42. Akenson, *God's Peoples*, 9.

43. As quoted in Akenson, *God's Peoples*, 14.

44. Ibid.

45. See Akenson, *God's Peoples*, 16 for details.

46. See the scriptural references cited in chapter four.

47. See Akenson, *God's Peoples*, 21.

48. As quoted in Akenson, *God's Peoples*, 26.

49. See Akenson, *God's Peoples*, 62–63 for details.

50. See Akenson, *God's Peoples*, chapter three for details.

51. See Akenson, *God's Peoples*, for details.

52. Ibid.

53. As quoted in Akenson, *God's Peoples*, 47.

54. Akenson, *God's Peoples*, 68.

55. As quoted in Akenson, *God's Peoples*, 69.

56. Ibid.

57. See Akenson, *God's Peoples*, 92–93 ff. for details.

58. See Akenson, *God's Peoples*, 94–95 ff. for details.

59. No doubt the victory of the African National Congress led by Nelson Mandela over the Afrikaner-led South African government at the end of the twentieth century will be interpreted by Afrikaners in South Africa within the same biblical framework.

*Chapter Four*

# THREE STRATEGIES IN THE QUEST FOR PURITY

As indicated by the last chapter, the quest for purity is an important theme characterizing the fundamentalist ethos and worldview. Because they regard the world as impure, fundamentalists face the problem of devising strategies to avoid that world or, alternatively, to confront and defeat it. Avoidance through flight is a fundamentalist reaction at one extreme; separation— physical, social, or symbolic—is a second reaction to an impure world; and militant struggle to overcome and capture that world is a third reaction. The quite different reactions of fundamentalists to a common problem again illustrates the fact that fundamentalists are tied not so much by a particular cultural content, but rather by their common orientation to the modern world: an orientation of outrage, protest, and fear.

Flight has long been a strategy pursued by minoritarian religious groups who suffer oppression, discrimination, or both. Perhaps the most famous western historical example is the Essenes, a sect/cult that fled from ancient Jerusalem to the caves overlooking the Dead Sea to meditate and pursue its own religious interpretations (the Dead Sea Scrolls). The Druze—a small religious group that arose in Fatamid Egypt, suffered persecution there, and fled to the mountains of Lebanon in the eleventh century—is an example from the Muslim tradition. And as described in chapter three, beginning in 1836, the Boers of South Africa (representing the Dutch Reform Church tradition) trekked 1,000 miles from Cape Province to the Transvaal to escape the pervasive secular influence brought by English settlers and administrators representing the British Empire.

The primary fundamentalist example of this strategy is the contemporary religious group "Excommunication and Flight" (*takfir wa hijra*), so named by the Egyptian press and public (the members named themselves "The Society of Muslims") because they declared excommunicated most Egyptian Muslims, whom they regarded as idolators. The group members made this declaration because they considered most Egyptian Muslims to have fallen away from religious piety, engaging, as they claimed, in usury, fornication, prostitution, the mixing of sexes in public, and the drinking of alcohol (Stella, a national beer, was very popular in Cairo). All this, they claimed, was done with the approval of the Sadat government. These fundamentalists referred to the corrupt version of Islam propagated by the government as the "*'ulema* (religious scholars) of the princes" and the religion of the state (*din al-dawla*). The authentic version, their own purified version of Islam that followed the Prophet's tradition (they shaved their heads, cultivated trimmed beards, and wore black cloaks after his example) was termed the religion of the people (*din al-milla*);[1] authentic Muslims attended (private) popular (*ahli*) mosques.

Early in the movement's development, it split into two parts, one of which pursued the strategy of violent confrontation with the government, resorting to the kidnapping of government ministers and assassination. Many of the leaders were caught, tried, and executed. The members of the other branch abandoned their urban residences for caves near the desert to escape the reach of the government and the pressure for conformity with the majority population of Muslims. Flight is also a demonstration of protest and sometimes defiance. It allowed this group of Egyptian fundamentalists to avoid common national obligations such as military conscription and payment of taxes.

Other branches of Excommunication and Flight resorted to radical social separation rather than physical flight. They remained within urban centers but formed their own "families" within these centers, living with like-minded fundamentalists of both sexes in crowded apartments. They prayed separately in these apartments, refusing to attend mosques led by government-appointed (and therefore contaminated) preachers. They taught their children in their own homes rather than send them to public schools whose curriculum they regarded as corrupting; furthermore, in their view all teachers in public schools were appointed by the corrupt central government. And they refused intermarriage with those who were not members of their own religious movement. When they did marry they refused to be married by mainline religious officials; that is, the usual religious specialists who served the majority population. In general, Excommunication and Flight protested against the secularization of society as well as its westernization: the introduction of western fashions for women and western entertainments for Muslim families (western films and television programs portraying amorous cross-sex relations) that violated Muslim norms of sobriety, modesty, and honor.

Another example of radical separation (but not flight) from an impure world is the case of the Reb Arelach *haredim*, referred to above, who live in the gated quarter of Mea Shearim in Jerusalem.[2] *Haredim* is a term Israelis use to designate those Jews who defend the faith and keep the law without making the kind of compromises to the secular world common to the majority in Israel. They maintain tradition when all around them do not. Outsiders designate them as the "ultraorthodox." But they designate themselves by the Yiddish term *erlicher Yidn*, which means virtuous Jews, not a sect of Judaism but the true Jews.[3] Like Excommunication and Flight, the *haredim* regard the central government of Israel with distrust and often hostility because they see that government as supporting a "permissive society" in which Judaism, particularly their law-conscious mystical interpretation, threatens to be overwhelmed by nightclubs, cinemas, television, immodesty of women (particularly their dress), hedonistic cross-sex relations, violation of kosher rules, and the secularization of education.

To ward off the powerful flow of impure culture that emanates from the government, secular Jews, and foreign countries, the *haredim* have gathered in their own quarter of Jerusalem, Mea Shearim, where they conduct their own way of life according to their own strict rules. They do not allow strangers to enter their quarter and strut their profane style of life with impunity. Immodestly dressed men and women who enter their quarter are heckled and sometimes stoned. Just before the Sabbath they close the gate to their quarter and permit no one in or out until the Sabbath ends twenty-four hours later. By this radical social and physical separation the *haredim* are able successfully to ward off the forces of the impure society that surround them.

When the Reb Arlech *haredim* leave their quarter, as they do when they go on pilgrimages to the shrines of Jewish saints or when they go on vacations, they maintain their physical and social separation (i.e., they remain encapsulated among the impure majority). Heilman recounts how they take vacations to points near and far:

> entire groups went to the Dead Sea, to their own separate beaches (where men and women remained segregated), took the cure and returned home. And even those who went abroad commonly went only to places where there were large concentrations of other *haredim*. Thus, when I traveled to Arosa, a village in the Swiss Alps, to see the *haredim* on vacation with their rebbe, I found a part of the town black with them: they had their own hotel where they sat and studied texts in between the meals and the thrice-daily prayer services. The hotel inside looked no different than their places back home. The setting might be Swiss, but the content was all *haredi* and Jewish. Even in the United States there are whole villages in the Catskill Mountains of upstate New York or the White Mountains of New Hampshire that are little more than transient twins of ultra-orthodox communities in Brooklyn.[4]

Wherever they appear outside their quarter, the *haredim* are immediately set off by their dress and appearance. They are always in black and white, with men distinguished by beards and ear locks and women with hair covered.

The BBA, as previously discussed, illustrates another strategy of separation, less radical than Excommunication and Flight and the *haredim* and based more on institutional and symbolic rather than physical and spatial separation. The school itself separates fundamentalists from others in addition to dress, language, and demeanor. The Bethany Baptist Academy (BBA) is a Christian academy in a city of 50,000 in Illinois. It was studied by an anthropologist who immersed himself in the activities of students, teachers, and administrators for one year.[5] In speaking with the author, the leader of the BBA outlined the posture of the school regarding the impure world of which it had to be a part:

The Bible says that we are in the world, but not to be of the world. . . . I want to reach the world, but I don't want to be identified as necessarily part of the world. We're the light of the world. Let's have no fellowship with those who live in darkness. We're not to be in partnership or relationship with the untruthful works of darkness. One way the Bible teaches us to convict them is by not having any fellowship with them.[6]

The BBA insisted that education be in Christian schools, with higher education outside such schools only if no Christian college were available. The academy urged students not to form close ties with non-Christians; not to date non-Christians; not to marry non-Christians; to prefer Christian candidates in the voting booth; and to carry back and apply their Christian ethics and Christian ethos in their homes. However, there was no Christian yellow page listing in the telephone book with names of preferred merchants and physicians, and BBA families had no restrictions placed on where they could live. Although certain occupations were preferred, beginning with "full-time Christian service" (i.e., the ministry or missionary service), with a small number of exceptions (bartender, gambler, rock musician, and movie picture projectionist), occupations were open. The BBA recognized that in general, contact with non-Christians could not be avoided and urged students to maintain "polite, sociable, and distant" relations while working among non-Christians.[7] It is important to note here that "non-Christians" designated all those who were "not saved" (i.e., had not received Jesus in the form of the Holy Spirit in their adult life). Therefore, the world of the impure was far larger than might first appear.

Because the BBA applied the principle of separation differently in different domains of culture, and because it did not constrain daily contact with nonbelievers in the workaday world, special devices were necessary to provide protection for the core believers. These devices were symbolic and ethical. On the symbolic side, a dress code sets Bethany students apart from others: short hair for boys, nice dresses and stockings for girls, and the absence of blue jeans for both. More important on the symbolic side is a whole vocabulary of salvation that defines the quest for divine grace as well as the degree of its achievement: "being saved," "grown in the Lord," "testifying," "witnessing," "full-time Christian," "born again," "the fallen faithful," "get in the word," "get right with the Lord," "the place the Lord wants you to be," and "we put the Lord first." In other words, separation is defined in spiritual terms: One has to be pure in heart and mind and to receive Jesus as Lord and Savior (i.e., one had to be "saved"). All these symbolic statuses or processes have ethical correlates. In other words, one must be one's brother's as well as one's own keeper. Each born-again Christian (nearly all students and teachers claimed that state) must occasionally "testify" (i.e., to make public statements in front of their coreligionists that contained confessions of sins and renewed spiritual commitments). They are continually asked to "witness," which means pronouncing their own firm belief to other nonmembers and urging them to come to church and open their hearts to the Holy Spirit (i.e., to proselytize). Students are constantly being monitored by their teachers and peers for signs of being "unsaved" (e.g., inappropriate language, inability to pray, ignorance of devotions). One symbolic spiritual status requires striving for the next: "being saved" requires giving up exuberant parties, but that status in turn leads to "being grown in the Lord" (i.e., to witnessing).

Because the BBA did not segregate its students from the world at large, it had to develop other devices to ensure effective inculcation of its message. Besides its elaborate vocabulary of degrees of salvation and their ethical correlates, and along with constant monitoring, it developed "total teaching" and strived for a "total atmosphere." Total teaching was introducing biblical lessons and religious messages in all classes including math and English. Furthermore, not just all classes but all school activities began with prayer (e.g., the bus driver or coach prayed before the bus left on its trip). Parents were constantly urged to support the teachings and the attitude of the BBA at home to produce the "total atmosphere" of Christianity that would embrace school, work, and home and produce "the full-time Christian." If parents were not as supportive as required, the student either withdrew or was expelled. Either way, by these devices the BBA was able to maintain its Christian standards while still living in the impure world.

At the higher educational level, the Christian academy is paralleled in the United States by the Christian college. Here again separation from the impure world is not so much spatial and physical as institutional and social. Bob Jones University in South Carolina is an example of such institutional separation, with students trained formally for evangelization (missionary work) but repudiating politicking (running for office, demonstrating, or forming national-level pressure groups). Again, separation is applied selectively in different domains. The rationale for political passivism is the same for the students at Bob Jones University as for the *haredim*: each group believes that a messiah will return to establish an earthly kingdom independent of any human (political) activity.

Munson's anthropological description of Hajj Muhammad, a Muslim fundamentalist in postcolonial Morocco gives us a better understanding of fundamentalist attitudes toward purity in a Muslim postcolonial context.[8] Although the Quran plainly states that the prophet Muhammad was nothing but a man, popular Muslim belief has held not only that the Prophet is pure and sinless, but also that these attributes attach to his direct descendants. In Morocco, one of the best ways to wash away one's sins is to make a pilgrimage to saints' tombs, saints who are regarded as being direct descendants of the Prophet.[9] Prayer also purifies. Hajj Muhammad said the following about the spiritual and emotional impact of daily prayers:

> When I hear the call to prayer, I go to the mosque. . . . And there I feel happy and clean. . . . The greatest part of the prayer is the touching of the floor with the forehead. The imam intones *Allahu akbar*, "God is greater." Then all the Muslims in the mosque respond *Allahu akbar* and prostrate themselves with their foreheads and palms on the floor, whispering *Subhana Rabbi al-ala*, "My Lord the most high be praised." The whole mosque is silent but for this whispered praise and supplication. . . . It is then, when the Muslim touches his forehead to the ground in utter submission and humility before God, that he is closest to Him. This is the best time for supplication, when the Muslim is lowest to the ground and closest to God the most high. This is the moment when the Muslim is purest and happiest and safest from the temptations of Satan.[10]

If prayer and pilgrimage and contact with the Prophet's descendants purifies, contact with infidels defiles. Hajj Muhammad is quite explicit on this matter too:

> I asked a Spanish shopkeeper for a glass of water. He said no and looked at me as if I were some kind of dirty animal that had no right to drink from the

glass of a Spaniard. I punched that Christian in the face and his white shirt was red from the blood of his nose. The Spanish soldiers put me in . . . jail for three days. The Christians think we are dirty, but they are dirty. That is why we do not allow them in our mosques. Whenever I work for a Christian or a Jew, I feel dirty and I go to the *hammam* [public steam bath]. But the cobblestone quarter is a clean neighborhood. . . . There are hardly any Christians or Jews in it now.[11]

Subsequently, Hajj Muhammad assaulted the Italian manager of a Spanish ice cream factory in Morocco after he declared that Muslims were stupid and dirty. He was tried by a "Christian judge" and jailed for six months. Two facts stand out from these incidents: the idiom of dialogue on both sides is purity and impurity and the mode of interaction is violent confrontation, physical and verbal.

The source of impurity is not always the foreigner or infidel. It is also the rich and powerful Moroccans who have abandoned their religion. Hajj Muhammad describes the richest man in his mountain village, Si Muhammad Qasim:

Si Muhammad Qasim used to have a lot of Spanish friends. They bought his pork—may God punish him for dealing in this polluted meat—and his honey. And they would come and stay in his house in the village and they would hunt wild boar and jackals together. Partridges and hares too. He was not ashamed to pollute his house and his village by the presence of infidels. It is enough that they pollute our cities. He had to pollute every house that he, his wife, and his children live in. I think he even took them to the holy tomb of Sidi Hbib [Saint Habib].[12]

What outraged Hajj Muhammad was the introduction of the foreigner and infidel into the inner sanctum of the family where the caretaker of purity, the woman (wife), became defiled by exposure, and into the inner sanctum of religion, the shrine of the descendant of the Prophet. It is important to note here that in Hajj Muhammad's worldview, the Spanish and French are not principally identified by their national or linguistic identity but by their religious identity: they are "Christians," "Jews," or "infidels." In addition to purity there is definitely a symbolic reference to power in these relationships. Hajj Muhammad makes this relationship explicit when recounting his work history to Munson:

And I worked as an apprentice . . . in a Spanish candy factory. Then I worked in a Spanish ice cream factory. . . . And then I worked for a Jew unloading bags of cement from trucks. The Muslim lives on the money of the Christian and the Jew. In this world they are always on the top and we are always on the bottom. But in the hereafter, God willing (*in sha' Allah*) we shall be on the top and they shall be on the bottom.[13]

Here we have accentuated the powerful anticolonial thrust of Muslim fundamentalism. When Munson did his study, Morocco had been an independent country for more than twenty-five years, but European influence continued pervasive culturally (in language, clothing styles, and urban entertainments) and economically (Europeans still ran the factories).

In my own research in the Jordanian village of Kufr al-Ma over a period of forty years (beginning in 1959), I have witnessed the transition from a mainline majoritarian view of purity to a more fundamentalist view. In that year I began reading the Quran with the preacher of the village with whom I cultivated a close relationship. The preacher allowed—really, invited—me to attend his Friday congregational sermons in the village mosque. I did so for more than a year and resumed doing so in 1965, 1966, and 1967. He never raised the question of ritual purity with me. Muslims are not allowed to enter the mosque or say their five daily prayers without performing ablutions (elaborate ritual purifications). In any case, based on the sermons I attended and recorded later in the preacher's house (fortunately, he wrote them out in Arabic in longhand and read them out to me slowly so that I could type a transliterated version), I wrote a book analyzing Muslim preaching within the context of a peasant society.[14] The preacher was always cordial to me in all my subsequent trips to the village and never suggested that I (being of Christian background) convert to Islam or perform ablutions before entering the mosque.

During one of my later periods of field research in the village in 1986, a well-known preacher who originated in the adjoining village but preached in town visited Kufr al-Ma. The preacher of Kufr al-Ma, as was the custom, asked him to deliver the Friday mosque sermon in his stead. He consented and was invited along with the village preacher and me to dinner in the house of a prominent villager immediately after the sermon and noon congregational prayers. When I entered the villager's house I overheard a number of the village's young men engaging the visiting preacher in rather heated debate. The subject of the debate was the propriety of the village preacher allowing me in the mosque when I had not performed the required ablutions. How could an unbeliever be allowed in the mosque in this circumstance? Would I not defile the mosque?

The visiting preacher replied that the prophet Muhammad had received a delegation of Christians from Najran in Arabia in his house and put them up overnight in the mosque, an annex of the Prophet's house in Medina. So how could I be banished from the mosque? It was clear, however, that a substantial number of villagers disapproved of my entering the mosque, particularly during the Friday congregational prayer. With respect to the question of ritual purity, the ethos of the village had changed from the relaxed attitude of the 1950s, 1960s, and 1970s to a more militant fundamentalist attitude in the 1980s and 1990s. It was during this latter period that I was approached for the first time by several of the young adult men of the village, invited for tea, told that I would be doomed to damnation, and urged to convert to Islam to avert that outcome.

In a number of examples, we have investigated the strategies of flight and separation in its various modes. The third strategy for dealing with impurity in any of its forms (ritual, commensal, ethical, politico-economic) is confrontation. This strategy was alluded to early on in the example of the faction of Excommunication and Flight that resorted to violence and assassination against the Egyptian state in the 1970s and 1980s. It has been mentioned in the reaction of the Moroccan Hajj Muhammad to the insults hurled by foreigners and infidels against Muslims. However, confrontation does not require violence. Preacher and televangelist Pat Robertson entered the 1984 Republican presidential primary, contesting the nomination for the presidency. He and the Christian Coalition that supported him were not content to adopt the strategy of Bob Jones and the BBA—to separate, to teach the living of the Christian life, and to win souls. He and his backers believed it was necessary to enter the political fray and capture the state; that is, win the presidency in order to implement fundamentalist principles.

Such political activism does not necessarily have to be fought at the national level. Indeed, most fundamentalists who adopt this strategy pursue it at the local level, such as the parents in Kanawha County, West Virginia, who objected to the selection of certain textbooks by the local school board. They proceeded to demonstrate, disrupt school board meetings, and run for school board positions to attempt to displace the current occupants.[15]

*Gush Emunim* (the Bloc of the Faithful), an Israeli fundamentalist political movement, provides an example of the confrontational strategy in the Jewish tradition. The Gush did not agree with the strategy of the *haredim*. Strict separation and intensive education would not achieve their goals. Only militant political action, in their case Jewish settlement of what they refer to as Judea and Samaria (what Palestinians regard as Palestine and most Americans call "the West Bank")—by force if necessary against the will of Palestinians and the Jewish state—would reclaim the Holy Land and prepare the way for the millennium.[16] This theme of activism and confrontation as a fundamentalist strategy will be pursued at greater length in the next chapter.

What should be noted in conclusion is that whereas the strategies pursued by fundamentalists to achieve their objectives are clear, the nuances within each strategy are many. Separation can be institutional and social, ethical, ritual, political, spatial, physical, symbolic, or some combination of these. Confrontation can involve war with the state on the one hand or cooperation with certain of its elements on the other. The religious leaders associated with *Gush Emunim* have cooperated with secularists and modernists in the settlement of the West Bank although they despise their principles. Confrontation, then, can even justify coalitions with groups with whom one is not only ideologically incompatible but also regards as evil.

## Notes

1. See Gilles Kepel, *Muslim Extremism in Egypt: The Prophet and Pharaoh* (Berkeley: University of California Press, 1984), chapter three for a detailed description of this fundamentalist movement in Egypt in the 1970s and 1980s.

2. See Heilman, *Defenders of the Faith*, for an excellent, detailed anthropological study of a fundamentalist Jewish community in Israel.

3. See Heilman, *Defenders of the Faith*, 12–13.

4. Heilman, *Defenders of the Faith*, 138.

5. See Peshkin, *God's Choice*, for an excellent, detailed anthropological description of a fundamentalist school in Illinois.

6. Peshkin, *God's Choice*, 9.

7. Peshkin, *God's Choice*, 270–71.

8. See Munson, *The House of Si Abd Allah*, for an intimate portrait and comparison of two Moroccan cousins, one a mainline Muslim woman and the other an adult fundamentalist Muslim man.

9. See Munson, *The House of Si Abd Allah*, 9–10.

10. Munson, *The House of Si Abd Allah*, 183.

11. Munson, *The House of Si Abd Allah*, 83.

12. Munson, *The House of Si Abd Allah*, 148–149.

13. Munson, *The House of Si Abd Allah*, 82–83.

14. See Antoun, *Muslim Preacher in the Modern World*, for details.

15. See Antoun, *Muslim Preacher in the Modern World*, 20–23 for details.

16. See Lustick, *For the Land and the Lord*, for details.

*C h a p t e r    F i v e*

# ACTIVISM AND TOTALISM

The Quran states, "Never will God change the condition of a people until they change it themselves" (13:11).[1] This quotation illustrates that fundamentalists are not against change; rather, they seek to change the world to one where their particular religious practices are implemented above all others. This verse provides the appropriate scriptural basis for the focus on activism and totalism, two key interconnected themes underlying much fundamentalist ideology. Whereas the last chapter focused on the fundamentalist strategies of separation and flight, this chapter focuses on the strategy of confrontation and militant struggle. A prominent thrust of many militant movements is to take religion out of the church, mosque, and synagogue and into the home, the schools, the markets and factories, into the streets and the walls along those streets (graffiti), into battlefields, banks, political campaigns, parliaments, universities, women's auxiliaries, and pioneering settlements. Fundamentalists are not fatalists. They believe in the "repair of the world,"[2] and in fighting back ideologically, socially, economically, symbolically, juridically, and politically. Whereas Muslims look to the Quran and the Traditions of the Prophet to legitimize an activist and totalist orientation, Christians and Jews look to the Bible/Torah/Talmud as a blueprint for everyday life.

Activism and totalism is a reaction to the ideology of modernism and the condition of modernity (see chapter one), in particular to the dominance of a secular society that separates religion from the dominant spheres of activity: the school, the marketplace and economic activity in general, the family, the legal system, the political arena, and the mass media.[3] This chapter indicates the range of political and legal activism, discusses the separation of the religion of the state from the religion of the people, and then illustrates the commitment to activism and totalism with five cases: one each from Iran, Israel, and Palestine, and two from the United States. In the course of doing so, the chapter explores fundamentalist activity on the battlefield, in the streets, in the church, in the mosque, at the ballot box, in the television studio, in the courtroom, in the school, and even in the cemetery!

## Political Activism

The fundamentalist-led Islamic rebellion in Algeria in the 1990s, for instance, was directed against a secular state and a secular society where schools are not segregated according to gender and western dance and music are accepted. Because it has had close ties with its former colonial occupiers, France, for more than 150 years, Algeria is more secular than other Arab countries. This is attested to by the wide dispersion of French television and radio, the immigration of many Algerians to work in France, and the frequent travel of Algerians to France.[4] The rebellion, led by the Islamic Salvation Front, aimed to turn Algeria into an Islamic republic. The fundamentalists entered the Algerian political arena with a vengeance in 1990 and won control of about eigth hundred municipalities in local elections, and in 1991 won a significant victory in elections for the Algerian parliament. Bearded men were seen accompanying their wives, daughters, and other female relatives to the polling places.[5]

When Israeli voters voted in a national election in November 1988, a picture of a Brooklyn rebbe (Jewish mystic leader and scholar) who had never been to Israel appeared in their voting cards. He exhorted them to vote for a major religious party, Agudat Israel:

> "The Rebbe is with row 3," the card declared over a picture of Menahem . . . Schneerson, the leader of the Lubavitch Hasidic group. An estimated 20,000 Jews in Brooklyn and tens of thousands around the world consider him their spiritual leader. . . . Israel's four religious parties . . . won a total

of 18 seats out of 120 in Parliament and are believed to hold the balance of power in forming the next government—Rabbi Schneerson and his followers are rejoicing . . . in the Crown Heights section of Brooklyn on Israel's election night.[6]

Those who voted for the designated party were blessed by the rebbe. Here is an example of fundamentalist activism in the political arena in the United States. In this case the activism is transnational.

In 1995 the Welfare Party, a militant Islamic group in Turkey, took control in elections in Ankara, the capital, and in Istanbul, the country's largest city. The party offers subsidized bread, health clinics, hostels for students, and other services that the central government cannot supply. This party has closed shelters for battered women, tried to segregate buses by gender, attacked ballet as a degenerate art form, and advocated that Istanbul's ancient walls be torn down as a symbol of Byzantine Christendom.[7] In 1997 the newly elected prime minister of the Welfare Party indicated that he wished to repeal laws that forbade female civil servants and students at public universities from wearing veils or head scarves; he is encouraging young people to study at religious academies and appointing Islamists to positions in many government agencies. Because secularism (the separation of religion and the state) is an essential part of the Turkish constitution since the modern Turkish state was established in the 1920s, many Turks in government and the army fear that the election of Turkish fundamentalists portends the fall of the secular state.

It is interesting that in Pakistan as well as Algeria and Turkey, Muslim parties place social legislation at the center of their electoral mandate: the withdrawal of women from the workforce unless absolutely necessary, the veiling of women and their segregation in schools and workplaces, and the repeal of secularist family laws making it more difficult for a man to divorce his wife unilaterally or to acquire a second wife. The Islamic parties contend that only Islam can govern such family practices as divorce and polygyny.[8]

In the United States a quite different example of radical confrontation with secular American society was presented by the legal indictment of a Jewish rabbi and his wife, who ran a Hasidic school, or yeshiva. They were charged with abducting a thirteen-year-old Jewish student who attended their school because they regarded his parents as secularists. They argued that according to Jewish law a boy, once bar mitzvahed (ritually confirmed in his adult status), "becomes a man capable of making his own decisions" (i.e., of pursuing a religious education regardless of his parents' wishes). They declared that the boy freely chose to continue his religious education against the parents' wishes.[9]

In Israel, where fundamentalist Jews remain a minority, they exercise extraordinary "political" influence, tipping the balance of power between the two dominant parties, Labor and Likud. They have prevailed on the national government to pass legislation exempting students in religious schools (yeshivas) from service in the army. Among their concerns is a "fear that they will find worldly lures in the army irresistible."[10] One rabbi referred to the fundamentalist drive for army deferment in the following way: "Now [without conscription] you're in control of his mindset [in a religious school], his religious life, his sex life, his marital life, his economic life. It's a total environment."[11] Fundamentalist Israelis also demand a change in Israel's law defining who is a Jew (to make it more restrictive) and "new laws to legislate the strict observance of the Jewish Sabbath."[12] They are reacting to the blatant nonobservance of the Sabbath in Tel Aviv where secularized Jews flock to nightclubs, movie theaters, restaurants where they eat pork, and bars attracting writers, musicians, business people, and college students, all in a mixed-gender environment.[13] All these initiatives, legislative and electoral, demonstrate political activism by fundamentalists.

## Legal Activism

Another domain of this totalistic activism is legal. The League for Concerned Women of America, with headquarters in Washington, D.C., and 573,000 members organized into 1,800 Prayer/Action Groups around the country, has a staff of six lawyers and a network of legal offices. The league has been involved in supporting seven families in rural Tennessee who sued their school system because they did not provide alternative textbooks for their children. The parents declared that the texts used in the schools emphasized themes that undermined their religious principles: pacifism, evolution, feminism, and disobedience of parents. The League for Concerned Women opposes abortion rights, sex education, condom advertising on television, and equal pay to men and women; it supports a strong military system, antiabortion legislation, mandatory AIDS blood testing for marriage license applicants, and antiobscenity laws.[14]

A more recent development on the Concerned scene is the establishment of "religious liberty law firms," operating out of the American Center for Law and Justice, the Rutherford Institute, the Becket Fund for Religious Liberty, and the Christian Legal Society Center for Law and Religious Freedom. These firms have argued cases up to the Supreme Court. Some of these law firms focus on crafting friend-of-the-court briefs, others on freedom of speech cases, and still others on litigation. They have defended Randall Terry, founder of Operation Rescue, in legal cases arising from abortion clinic protests. When allegations of violations of religious liberty are received, "SWAT teams" (lawyers who fly across the country to confront offending school principals or city councils) are sent out.[15]

In the Muslim World, the tendency toward legal totalism and activism is illustrated by the increasing scope of "fatwas," religious interpretations by Muslim scholars of particular issues brought to them by ordinary people. Fatwas have increasingly been used in a political context for and against religious activists. Since the 1980s certain interpreters of Muslim scripture and Muslim law ("muftis") have increasingly added to their usual rendering of interpretations on matters of worship and social relations (e.g., religious fasting, marriage, divorce, and charitable obligations). The have added interpretations on matters contested in the political and public arena. For instance, they have considered whether peace with Israel is sanctioned by scripture and religious law, whether suicide bombing and hostage taking in war is allowed, and whether particular films and books should be banned.[16]

A particular aspect of activism in the political–legal realm is constitutional. In Egypt, largely because of pressure from fundamentalists, a clause in the Egyptian constitution saying Islamic law was "one of the sources of legislation" was changed in 1979 to read, "Islam is the religion of the state, Arabic is its official language and principles of Islamic law are its main sources of legislation."[17]

Banking and the taking of interest is another focus of Muslim activists. In 1992 Pakistan's highest Islamic court declared that all forms of interest (*riba*) on bank loans, deposits, and international borrowing and lending were "repugnant" to Islam and ruled that Pakistan must abolish such interest by June. The prime minister had been elected on a platform of bringing "Islam in all of its facets fully into the life of the country."[18] A commission on the Islamization of the Economy was established to devise rules for financial transactions without interest. Businessmen in Pakistan feared that state planning, free market privatization, and large public work projects financed by international lending based on interest would be jeopardized. Saudi Arabia on the other hand, which enforces Islamic law in many spheres, sidestepped the issue by calling interest "profit" or "service charges."[19]

Another important domain of activism is the home. In the large city of Tashkent in Central Asia a mullah (low-level religious scholar, preacher, or prayer leader) stated that he came to the mosque to worship and not to preach. He felt safe preaching "only in the homes of believers, where the risk of police surveillance is reduced." He further stated: "There are two kinds of mullahs. There are the official, the approved mullahs. And there are the underground mullahs like myself. We don't preach in mosques. We preach in people's homes. Now there are many more fundamentalists than official mullahs."[20]

The political, legal, constitutional, financial, and kinship domains mentioned above illustrate the "totalistic" range of fundamentalist activity. They demonstrate that for activist fundamentalists, religion is not confined to the church, mosque, or synagogue.

## The Religion of the State and the Religion of the People

The mullah's statement leads us to an important phenomenon in many societies where fundamentalists contend for power and influence, particularly in Muslim societies: the distinction between "official religion," or the "religion of the state," and "the people's religion" (*din al-dawla* versus *din al-milla*). For instance, in Tunisia the incoming president, Ben Ali, who came to power in a coup d'état, immediately set a new tone by invoking "Allah [God], the compassionate and the merciful," to justify his coup. Subsequently he had himself filmed at prayers in the mosque and made the pilgrimage to Mecca. The call to prayer is now broadcast five times a day on television, and the broadcast of a major European championship soccer game (an extremely popular sport in Tunisia) was interrupted so that a prayer leader "could intone the official start of Ramadan" (the month of fasting). Tunisian soccer players (who are government sponsored) now sometimes cover their knees out of deference to the Islamic norm of modesty. The president also created an office of religious affairs. All of this is part of official (state) Islam.[21]

In Egypt the central government's change of the constitution to make Islam the religion of the state and its sponsorship and control of numerous "official mosques" (i.e., those in which government-appointed preachers and prayer leaders officiate) allows it to claim that it is a champion of religion.[22] In the 1970s—to counteract the despised religion of the state—fundamentalists at the University of Minya in southern Egypt sought to reclaim secular space for the religion of the people by encroaching on an open public area between the colleges of Arts and Education and establishing a mosque (a permanent prayer ground) there. When the police expelled them from the grounds, they held a Friday congregational prayer in the middle of the street on a busy bridge across the Nile, disrupting traffic for some time. They also carved out for themselves "Islamic zones" within the university: their own bulletin boards, sections of the cafeteria, and rest areas.[23] In prerevolutionary Iran the sharp demarcation between state-run/controlled mosques and popular mosques is similar to Egypt and Tashkent in Central Asia where the mullah was afraid to preach in the official mosque. In Algeria the central government arrested more than forty-two imams, or religious leaders, and banned political activity (i.e., controversial preaching) in popular mosques.[24]

In the United States fundamentalist movements and organizations distinguish themselves from religious groups they believe to be reflective of the social and religious establishment, for example, the National Council of Churches. In all these countries fundamentalists deride the claims and purported "religious" behavior of presidents, prime ministers, parliaments, and religious leaders of establishment groups. As the fundamentalist mullah in Tashkent put it, "So you see there are Muslims in word and Muslims in deed."[25] Fundamentalists see themselves as the true believers and the proponents of official religion as hypocrites who advance a superfluous brand of religion and use it for their own purposes.

## The Battlefield

A final domain of fundamentalist activism is the battlefield, elaborated in various ways as civil insurrection, assassination, or terrorism. In Egypt militant Muslims have killed government officials, police officers, and occasionally tourists; they have tossed firebombs at liquor stores and bars and attacked Christian shops and churches. Between 1992 and 1994, 290 people were killed and 670 wounded as the militants—admittedly a small minority—fought to replace the government of President Mubarak with a strict Islamic state.[26] In November 1979 militant Muslims in Saudi Arabia assaulted the Grand Mosque in Mecca and occupied it for two weeks before they were driven out by Saudi forces. Heavy fighting between government forces and more than 700 militants resulted in 244 deaths on both sides. The attackers struck during dawn hours and took about fifty hostages, including many Saudi government officials. They demanded that their leader be recognized as the religious redeemer of the age.[27]

Algeria is the locus of perhaps the most violent militant struggle. From early 1992 until summer 1999 it was reported that 100,000 people died. The seven years of insurgency produced another million victims, including the wounded and those who lost homes or relatives.[28] Of course, probably half these casualties were perpetrated by government forces and half by fundamentalists in an increasingly violent civil war. The civil war was initiated by the secularist central government dominated by army officers who cancelled the results of 1991 parliamentary elections—results that had brought fundamentalists to political power. The leaders of the Islamic Salvation

Front initially aimed at "wearing down the state's apparatus through constant demonstrations, strikes and civil disobedience."[29] The front's official slogan is, "No Constitution and no laws [both deemed to be the products of a corrupt secular state]. The only rule is the Koran and the law of God."[30]

The previous year the prime minister had postponed the first multiparty parliamentary elections to be held in Algeria and declared a state of emergency following two weeks of fundamentalist street protests in which nineteen people were killed and two hundred wounded. A new high security council, including three top generals, was formed to organize the government's effort to crush the militants. The Algerian civil war continues as the next century begins in a classic confrontation of "official Islam" (government religion) and popular Islam (as evidenced by the election of the Islamic Salvation Front to power in free elections). Official Islam argues that "religion is a personal matter and that there is no point to a political party that says some Muslims are better than others."[31] Popular Islam argues for the application of Islamic norms to all domains of culture, including an Islamic state.

The struggle in Algeria is also a struggle over which culture, Arabic or French, should prevail in Algeria. Islamic militants have fought to eradicate all vestiges of France in Algeria including ending all foreign language education and French models of administration, health, management, consumer patterns, military organization, and law enforcement—all ingrained in the fabric of Algerian life as a result of more than a hundred years of French colonial control. Can Muslim fundamentalists uproot French culture and the French language when French is a lingua franca for nearly all educated Algerians and when four million Algerian migrants work in France, Spain, or Italy? As an incisive reporter pointed out, "Most Algerians are under 25. They don't remember France [whose political control in Algeria ended in 1962]. Their identity is Islamic, not imitation European."[32] Such are the cultural roots of the clash between fundamentalists and official Islam.

Although many foreign observers have feared that a victory of Islamic militants in Algeria harbingers an Iranian-style fundamentalist state, they "overlook the fact that many of the Algerians who voted it [Islamic Salvation Front] into power, including many of the poor and devout, are totally turned on to Europe. . . . Western Europe which lies just across the Mediterranean Sea . . . remains the stuff of which Algerian dreams are made."[33] Flashy European television programs are seen in more than 60 percent of Algerian homes. The educated elite has a love–hate relationship with France and its culture because although the French killed one and one-half million Algerians in their colonial war against Algerian independence, they left the French language, which nearly all Algerians speak, and French newspapers, which half the population reads.[34]

Iran, on the other hand, has been called "the island of particularism" (i.e., a land isolated from other cultures, particularly from European cultures, by distance and two substantial mountain chains), a land that has focused in on itself and its own distinctive Shi'ah Muslim culture. European models inspire only a small Iranian elite. Moreover, the (Shi'ah) version of Islam practiced in Iran is itself minority Islam. Very few Iranians have had any contact with Europe. Despite the increasingly brutal Algerian civil war that has victimized foreigners, journalists, native Algerian villagers, and urbanites, there is no way that Islamic fundamentalism in Algeria could ever replicate Islamic fundamentalism in Iran.

## The Iranian Revolution and the Shi'ah Ethos and Worldview

Let us now consider perhaps the most dramatic case of fundamentalist activism in the twentieth century, the Iranian Revolution. It has been said that the Iranian Revolution is a model case of a religious revolution: secular nationalism was its stipulated enemy; its critique of secular government and secular society was in a religious idiom; led by religious figures, it provided a vision of an Islamic state.[35] However, the origins of the revolution and the forms it took at several stages were quite different than other fundamentalist movements and were rooted in a Shi'ah Muslim ethos and worldview that we must first understand.

In her book *The Battle for God*, Karen Armstrong argued that Iranian Shiism is motivated by two passions: social justice and "the Unseen [al-ghayb]." The Unseen refers to the spiritual world most explicitly symbolized in Shi'ah theology by the belief that the twelfth, or "Hidden Imam" (a direct descendant of the prophet Muhammad and the last of a long line of Shi'ah spiritual leaders), did not die back in the tenth century but rose to heaven and returns to earth from time to time to speak to his followers.[36] For Armstrong a myth is a primordial event that gives a people a way of looking at their society with a deep, timeless level of meaning, and of developing their interior spiritual lives, at the same time that it supplies a context for making sense of people's everyday lives.[37] Myth, far from being considered false or having to do with a faraway time and place, is a vital force with immediate implications for many domains of culture for the people who embrace it.

Whereas Sunni Muslims embraced a myth focused on the life of the Prophet, Shi'ah Muslims embraced a myth focused on his descendants. The myth of occultation of the twelfth imam (who had to go into hiding as described above), and the myth of the intercession of Husayn, the grandson of the Prophet and the third imam, expresses the ethos of Iranian Shi'ah society: an alienation from society and particularly from government, which is regarded as unjust and illegitimate.[38] According to the Shi'ah myth nearly all the twelve imams, who were direct descendants of the Prophet, died by violent means such as poisoning, assassination, and imprisonment (or in the case of Husayn, on the battlefield at Kerbala) at the hands of the secular governments of their day. These governments could no longer be trusted. This fact alone justified the dominant Iranian Shi'ah view of the "incompatibility of religion and politics."[39] Religious scholars and pious men were expected to refrain from government service, and ordinary people "had to cooperate with the powers that be."[40]

When anthropologist Mary Hegland went to conduct fieldwork in Iran in a village outside the city of Shiraz in southwestern Iran in 1978, at the beginning of the year of revolution, she discovered religious devotions oriented toward Husayn, the grandson of the Prophet and the third imam, that focused on his role as intercessor between human beings and God. Women usually went to a shrine of one of the imams and their descendants (imamzadeh) commonly found outside each village, and prayed for Husayn to intercede for them with God for some worldly purpose (e.g., for a barren woman to bear a child, for a son to succeed in his school exams, for a brother to be cured of some disease). No one ever participated in any confrontational political activity or spoke about possibly doing so.[41]

During the course of the revolution, a new understanding of the myth of Husayn—an activist fundamentalist view—was propagated and took hold. It was pointed out that back in the seventh century, Husayn was in the midst of carrying out his worship obligations in the performance of the Pilgrimage to Mecca (*hajj*); he was actually circumambulating the Ka'ba when word came to him from his adherents in Iraq that they needed his support because they were surrounded by the army of the powerful caliph in Damascus, Yezid, who threatened to destroy them. Husayn broke off the Pilgrimage, one of the five required pillars of Islam, and rushed to Iraq where he, his family, and followers were martyred. The reinterpretation of the myth was clear: Husayn was a revolutionary who believed that struggle against oppression was even more important than performance of the basic Muslim worship obligations. As the year wore on an increasing number of villagers studied by Hegland, women as well as men, accepted the activist interpretation of Husayn's mission and role in the world: they began participating in increasing numbers in demonstrations against the Shah in the neighboring city of Shiraz.[42]

This reinterpretation of Shi'ah Islam from a passive, apolitical religion of prayer and intercession to an activist one of defiance of state oppression was reflected over many months in 1978 and 1979 throughout Iran. Iranians demonstrated in a cycle of forty-day religious mourning ceremonies, beginning on August 1, 1978, when the Shah's forces fired on demonstrating students in the religious shrine center of Qum, killing seventy.[43] Iranian Shi'ah Islam stipulates major mourning ceremonies for the deceased after the fortieth day of death. Forty days after the initial deaths, mourning demonstrations took place in other cities. Again the Shah's forces retaliated by killing more demonstrators. Forty days later similar scenes resulted with similar results, and this forty-day cycle continued throughout the revolution. Although all demonstrators were not fundamentalists or even Shi'ah (the great majority were), all understood the symbolism of martyrdom and mourning transformed into the symbolism of resistance.[44] And all recognized the religious rhythm of revolutionary activity. Frequently, demonstrations began in cemeteries, a customary Shi'ah religious gathering place of family members come to commemorate the passing of kin. Now, however, instead of mourners beating their chests with their open palms or flagellating themselves with chains (as was usually done on these religious occasions, particularly during the month of Muharram, the occasion for the commemoration of the martyrdom of Husayn at Kerbala in Iraq), they were now demonstrators who marched with a clenched fist chanting, "Death to the Shah!" Other demonstrators yelled, "Everywhere is Kerbala and everyday is Ashura" (the tenth day of Muharram on which Husayn was killed), indicating a call to arms rather than a mourning ritual.[45]

The climax of the revolutionary religious demonstrations occurred in Tehran on December 10, 1978, on the Day of Ashura itself when two million demonstrators marched for eight hours, carrying green, red, and black flags, symbolizing Islam, martyrdom, and Shi'ah, respectively. They also carried banners reading, "We will kill Iran's dictator."[46] At the end of the demonstration a resolution was passed. Ayatollah Khomeini was invited to become the new leader of Iran and Iranians were urged to band together until the Shah was overthrown.[47]

After the return of Khomeini to Iran in February 1979 and the formation of the Islamic Republic, this totalist/activist worldview and ethos expressed itself in many domains: the reestablishment of Islamic law in the legal arena; the establishment of the institutions of the "[religious] just ruler" and the "[religious] Council of Guardians" in the political arena; the reinstitution of religious instruction in the educational arena; the extirpation of "Westoxification" in the social arena (including the institution of norms for the veiling of women, a ban on alcohol and gambling, and the censoring of all newspapers, films, and television broadcasts for sexually explicit content);[48] and in the national arena the merging of the Iranian nation-state with religious ideology through the depiction of national enemies such as the United States and the Shah as "the Great Satan" and "Pharaoh," respectively, and such national heroes as Khomeini as "Moses."[49]

# Hamas

We will now examine two cases of activism/totalism, one Palestinian, the other Israeli/American. These examples not only demonstrate activism and totalism in other milieus, but also pose the question of how and why certain religious confrontations become violent among certain fundamentalist followers who preach and practice martyrdom. The first is *Hamas*, a Palestinian organization founded by a quadriplegic religious leader, Shaykh Ahmed Yassin, in 1987 in the Gaza strip. *Hamas* is an Arabic acronym for "Islamic Resistance Movement" and also means zeal or fervor.[50] It emerged as a movement out of the broader religious movement known as the Muslim Brotherhood, which was founded in 1928 in Egypt to resist the British occupation. It must be noted that since its inception, the Muslim Brotherhood has operated in many different domains—welfare, education, underground armed struggle, worship (mosques), and missionary activity—and *Hamas* has continued that tradition. It runs boys' clubs, medical clinics, Quran schools, and kindergartens; at the same time separate wings of the organization conduct violent assaults on both civilian and military targets in Israel. *Hamas* has offices in Iran, Jordan, Syria, Libya, and Lebanon and a reputed underground leadership cadre in Europe and the United States. The organization is said to receive large amounts of money from abroad, particularly from legitimate business people in the Persian Gulf region, but it also expects and receives contributions from its own members. Thus, although its membership is located overwhelmingly in Palestine (Gaza and the West Bank), it is a transnational Muslim movement with links to fundamentalist movements in Algeria, the Sudan, and Tunisia.

Organizationally, *Hamas* is divided into four sectors, three in the West Bank and one in Gaza, each with its own leadership structure. In each sector "*da'wa* [literally translated, "call," i.e., missionary] groups" composed of lay Muslims act as its shock troops in such activities as establishing schools, imposing and monitoring moral standards (including banning alcohol and encouraging veiling), and disseminating religious literature.[51] The membership of *da'wa* groups is drawn from preachers, teachers, students, union leaders, and university graduates of the Islamic

University in Gaza.[52] A second level of organization is the "Youth Organization," established in 1988 with the beginning of the *Intifada* ("The Uprising"). The Youth Organization's "task was to resist the Israeli occupation by staging demonstrations, attacking Israeli troops with stones, distributing leaflets and writing revolutionary slogans on walls."[53]

The military wing of *Hamas*, the "*Qassam* Brigades," came into operation in 1990. Its initial aim was to target only Israeli soldiers, but after the 1994 Hebron massacre in which a Jewish settler killed more than forty Palestinians during Friday prayers, it widened its attack to include Israeli civilians.[54] The brigades were named after a Syrian religious leader, Izzedine al-Qassam, who fought the French, the British, and the Jews of Palestine in the 1920s and 1930s. He was regarded by his followers as the first Muslim leader to bring together the ideas of "Islam and revolution in armed struggle."[55] Members of the *Qassam* Brigades, who are said to be fewer than one hundred, receive orders only in coded messages with little face-to-face contact. Most of these *Hamas* militants try to fight to the death so as not to survive for interrogation.[56]

This well-organized, disciplined, well-financed group with a membership that crosscuts different classes was driven to violence first by the grassroots Palestinian Uprising in 1987 and second by the Oslo peace agreements in 1993 (and the Camp David peace agreements before them). Many Palestinians felt that the uprising and the agreements bypassed them and rendered peace without justice. This conclusion is a result of the fact that the Palestinians remained economically impoverished, politically powerless (without an Islamic state), and geopolitically and socially fragmented by Israeli settlements, roads that surrounded them patrolled by Israeli police, and continued harassment of Palestinians by Israeli settlers and by the Israeli bureaucracy and army. With the Oslo accord the *Qassam* Brigades began a series of kidnappings, suicide car bombings, and killings.

The Israeli government retaliated by arresting and banishing leaders (Shaykh Izzadine was jailed in 1989 and 415 *Hamas* activists were banished to Lebanon in 1992); by demolishing the houses of the extended families of activists suspected of perpetrating violence or sealing them in pursuit of the policy of collective punishment; and by killing activists in raids on homes and mosques organized by security forces.[57]

The ultimate activism of martyrdom must be examined more closely.[58] In Gaza instead of pictures of athletes or movie stars on the walls of homes, one frequently sees pictures of gunmen and suicide bombers. Their images are also carried in wallets and on key chains, and the "walls [along streets] are covered with graffiti saluting them and with bold drawings of their attacks."[59] What explains this adulation and the willingness of young Palestinian men to sacrifice themselves? One cannot understand it unless one understands the Muslim fundamentalist worldview, or at least the version of it accepted by some members of *Hamas*. In that view the present life is paltry, undignified, and dishonorable because it involves the continued humiliation of living under occupation (with Israeli-controlled checkpoints, curfews, and work permits); of being unable to provide for one's family; of being unable to educate one's children; or even being unable to pursue manual, not to mention professional, work in an uninterrupted manner. One man, married with children, said, "We're dead now. We live when the pieces of our bodies are collected in Tel Aviv."[60] Another suicide bomber told a reporter, "The life of this world is just a game and an accumulation of possessions and children. What God has is better for me than all this. I am sad to leave you, but let me meet God. I love paradise more than this world."[61]

Passages of the Quran suggest that martyrs sit next to God with other righteous men, and they enjoy multiple virgin brides.[62] Another prospective martyr wrote before he died, "Life is beautiful, but the more beautiful life is to be a martyr. Paradise is a delicious drink. Our enemies love life, but we adore death, so I am sacrificing my soul and everything I own to God."

Let us examine the portrait of a *Hamas* martyr. On February 25, 1996, Majdi Abu Warda, an eighteen-year-old man from an extended family of twenty, boarded a Jerusalem bus and lit a satchel packed with dynamite, killing himself and twenty-five passengers.[63] Majdi's profile fits that of other *Hamas* martyrs and includes the following attributes: potential bombers usually have a relative who was "killed, wounded or jailed during the occupation;"[64] typically they have a particular "long-standing frustration" such as trouble finding a bride or suffering shame for being afraid to throw stones at Israeli soldiers; they are generally between the ages of eighteen and twenty-four and unmarried, childless, and unemployed; they are capable of great self-discipline, sometimes revealed in the hobbies they pursue; and they come from families that are pious, regular readers of the Quran, though not zealots. Majdi never watched television and went to bed by eight every night.[65]

The preparation for the suicide bombing attack followed a certain modus operandi. Recruitment is usually from some kind of school or training center run by *Hamas*. Majdi was recruited from a vocational training center in Hebron where he was learning tile laying. Students are assigned various tasks to test their commitment; for example, delivering a gun or being buried in a mock grave. Then they are organized in cult-like groups of five to ten where they become mentally isolated from friends and family. They leave for their bombing missions straight from mosques where they have spent several days chanting the Quran with verses that give them a powerful sense of their own salvation. So strong is their conviction that "the bombers move in crowded places among Israelis without exhibiting any anxiety."[66]

The recruits know that *Hamas* will take good care of their families should they die. Families of martyrs receive $800 a month for life, scholarships for siblings, and subsidized rice. This is quite a substantial compensation for a poor family. If the family houses are demolished by the Israeli army in retaliation, *Hamas* pays for a replacement.[67]

But the significant rewards for martyrs are psychological or soteriological (gaining salvation), depending on one's worldview. The suicide bomber's death is described by militants as "the martyr's wedding" (i.e., an occasion of joy and celebration). The martyr is said to become a saint and sit next to God in heaven. His family takes pride in his supreme achievement and receives the esteem of the community.

## Dr. Baruch Goldstein and Rabbi Meir Kahane

Let us now examine a case of violent activism among Jewish fundamentalists. On February 25, 1994, Dr. Baruch Goldstein, a thirty-seven-year-old resident of Qiryat Arba (a Jewish settlement in the heart of the

Palestinian Hebron region) and a follower of Rabbi Meir Kahane, opened fire with an automatic weapon on Muslim worshipers attending the weekly Friday congregational worship in the mosque at the Shrine of the Patriarchs in Hebron. This site is revered by both Muslims and Jews because Abraham is believed to be buried there. Goldstein picked the only place in the world where both Muslims and Jews prayed, although they so do in separate but adjacent areas in the shrine. More than 50 Palestinians were killed and more than 150 wounded. Goldstein was finally overcome and killed by the enraged worshipers.[68]

Goldstein was one of thousands of New Yorkers who have moved from Brooklyn and Queens to Israel where they have become part of the settler movement that began after 1967 when Israel captured the Palestinian territories now referred to as "the West Bank" (of the Jordan River). Americans have always comprised a disproportionate percentage of Jewish settlers (approximately 120,000 in 1994) on the West Bank—perhaps 15 percent—and they made up an overwhelming percentage of the followers of Rabbi Meir Kahane's Kach Movement, of which Goldstein was a key member.[69] The ties between Rabbi Kahane and Goldstein and between the Jewish Defense League in Brooklyn and Queens and the Kach Movement in Israel are other dramatic examples of transnational religion and fundamentalism. In Kiryat Arba Goldstein served on the local council as the representative of the Kach Party.[70]

Goldstein was born in Brooklyn in the middle-class community of Bensonhurst in an orthodox Jewish family that kept apart from its neighbors, who were mainly secular Jews and Italians. His education was strictly orthodox including the Yeshiva of Flatbush, Yeshiva University, and the Albert Einstein College of Medicine where he was an exemplary student, graduating summa cum laude in 1981.

"He was always political," said a coreligionist who knew him in Brooklyn, stating that he brought speakers from Rabbi Kahane's movement to speak at places of worship.[71] Goldstein expressed his devout belief that Arabs were an intrusion into the land of Israel. At the end of a letter he wrote to the New York Times in June 1981, referring to the necessity to expel "the Arab minority from within its borders," he said, "Israelis will soon have to choose between a Jewish state and a democratic one."[72]

His religiopolitical mentor, Rabbi Meir Kahane, had founded the Jewish Defense League in Brooklyn in 1968 to patrol Jewish working-class neighborhoods that had been shifting toward African American and Hispanic majorities, with whom they were at odds. The members of the league escorted Jewish teachers through black neighborhoods with baseball bats, taught riflery and karate to rabbinical students, and invaded Soviet diplomatic offices to protest the treatment of Jews in the Soviet Union.[73]

Kahane later distributed .22-caliber rifles to patrols in East Flatbush. He preached that "western democracy as we know it is incompatible with Zionism" and that Jewish ritual law forbade close contact with non-Jews.[74] Rabbi Kahane was sentenced to a year in jail for conspiring to make bombs after a number of violent anti-Soviet attacks. It was Rabbi Kahane "who broke the taboo on discussing the expulsion of Arabs from Israel," opening the way for Israeli nationalist politicians and (later) settler leaders such as Dr. Goldstein.[75] In 1985 he wrote, referring to himself, " Kahane knows that there are no partial answers to the Arab threat. Kahane knows that only expulsion, ridding the land of them will save Israel."[76] In 1971 he moved to Israel and founded the Kach Party that espoused the same principles; "*Kach*" is literally translated as "Thus so!" connoting "Don't argue with me."

According to friends, Goldstein was not simply an admirer of Rabbi Kahane, he was a close associate who traveled with him in Israel and helped to organize Kach in the 1980s. Goldstein immigrated to Israel in 1983, and in 1984 ran Kahane's successful campaign for Parliament. He had become increasingly angered by the Middle East peace effort and by violence aimed by "Arabs" (to refer to them as "Palestinians" would give them legitimacy) at militant West Bank settlers.[77]

Both Goldstein's and Kahane's fundamentalist worldviews were anchored in the scripturally rooted covenant relationship found in the Torah, in which God promises the Land of Israel to the People of Israel (the ancient Hebrews) and their descendants, unconditionally in their interpretation.[78] In this view all history between ancient covenantal time and present time is irrelevant, thereby erasing the claims of Muslims to the holy land. That this covenantal time dominated Goldstein's view is attested to by his selection of the Shrine of the Patriarchs as the site of his retaliation, as has been suggested, for the assassination of Kahane, purportedly by an Egyptian Muslim in New York in 1990.[79] Goldstein's act was one of confrontation and defiance of Muslim claims to worship at the most sacred Jewish shrine after the Sacred Temple Enclosure in Jerusalem (which is also contested by Muslims who regard it as a sacred enclosure, or *haram*, and the site of Muhammad's ascent to heaven and conversation with God).[80] The dominance of covenantal or scriptural time in the views of Kahane, Goldstein, and other militant Jews is also reflected in their reference to the non-Jewish population of Israel by the scriptural term "Amalekites"—the hated enemies of the ancient Hebrews on whose heads God commanded Joshua to rain death and destruction—rather than as Palestinians or Arabs.[81]

The discussion of the last two cases, the militant wing of *Hamas* and the militant Kach Party, raises the question of why certain fundamentalists turn the strategy of confrontation into violence. Juergensmeyer has placed this question in a broader perspective, asking a broader question: Why does religion often lead to violence? He points out that much religious imagery is symbolically violent (e.g., the bloody conquests of the Hebrew Bible, the crucifixion of Jesus in Christianity, the martyrdom of Husayn in Shi'ah Islam, the awful battles fought in such Hindu epics as the Maharabata, and the sacrifice of Guru Tegh Bahadur in Sikhism).[82]

The actual commission of religious violence in acts that others term "terrorism" is also deliberately symbolically violent; that is, it is dramatic, often shocking, and designed "to elicit feelings of revulsion and anger."[83] Such acts are done to demonstrate a point. What is that point? For true believers and particularly for fundamentalists, the point is that the struggle is between good and evil. It is, then, a cosmic struggle and the vocabulary of such a struggle is used (e.g, "Great Satan," "Pharaoh," "Moses," *jihad* [holy war]).[84] Religious violence in its cosmic frame involves both sacrifice and war. Juergensmeyer argues that the framing of religious activity in a religious cosmos leads naturally to images of warfare and the behavior that follows. Religion is all about the imposition of order over disorder. Religious perspectives "assert the primacy of meaning in the face of chaos."[85] The rituals of sacrifice (i.e., martyrdom) are "enactments of cosmic war."[86] The foe, for *Hamas*—for Kach, for Khomeini, for Pat Robertson—is not a worldly foe, but a cosmic foe, and the struggle is not of today or yesterday but for all time and for one's salvation. It is not strange then that religious confrontations sometimes lead to violence.

## The New Christian Right and Ballot or Media Activism

We now turn away from the battlefield to an entirely different domain of fundamentalist activism: the mass media, particularly television and radio. The instance to be described involves the New Christian Right (NCR) in the United States. The NCR emerged around 1980 as a significant national movement that brought together television evangelists, renegade mainline clergymen, nascent leaders of single-issue lobbies, and numerous coordinating committees into three nationwide organizations: Christian Voice, the Religious Roundtable, and the Moral Majority.[87] One scholar, Hammond, has analyzed the movement in terms of "another great awakening," of which there have been several in the United States throughout the last 250 years. He posits five stages in such movements: crisis in legitimacy; personal distress interpreted as institutional failure leading to a nativist movement; creation of a new worldview; the restructuring of old institutions; and finally the absorption of the majority of the population in the new worldview.[88] He argues that the emergence of the NCR around 1980 represents the second stage of such a movement, which he goes on to define:

> There almost always arises a nativist or traditionalist movement within the culture, that is, an attempt . . . to argue that the danger comes from the failure of the populace to adhere more strictly to old beliefs, values and behavior patterns. . . . [The nativists'] solution is double-edged. First, they call for a return to the 'old-time religion,' 'the ways of our fathers,' and 're-spect for the flag' (or other symbols of the old order). Second, they tend to find scapegoats in their midst . . . upon whom they can set an example of revived authority (Mcloughlin, 1978, 14).[89]

The Christian Voice focused on secular issues; for example, developing morality ratings for congressmen not only on religious issues (prayers in the schools, Internal Revenue Service [IRS] rulings on Christian schools, abortion) but also on busing, economic sanctions against Rhodesia, behavioral research funding, and parental rights.[90] This activity was a forerunner of the later Christian Coalition's development of elaborate "Voter Guides" that listed the voting record of each congressional representative on issues of interest. The Christian Voice also conducted voter registration campaigns and endorsed candidates from the pulpit.

The Moral Majority, founded by the minister and televangelist Jerry Falwell in 1979, had the aim of establishing nationwide coalitions composed of Protestants, Catholics, and Jews who support conservative causes. Falwell traveled to all fifty states where he conducted "I Love America" rallies, aiming to set up local chapters in every state visited. His organization was dominated by clergymen with few lay leaders.[91] In the 1980 national election Falwell outrightly urged Protestant preachers to make political statements: "What can you do from the pulpit? You can register people to vote. You can explain the issues to them. And you can endorse candidates, right there in church on Sunday morning."[92]

Falwell did not think that such activity would threaten the tax exemption received from the IRS, which presumed that churches were nonpolitical organizations. He did not believe he was endorsing candidates: "I'm not saying [the Republican] Jerry Ford was the perfect candidate in 1976 but he was better than the other guy. I told my people in church how I was going to vote. We held a straw poll two weeks before the election and it turned out 97 percent for Ford, and you know that's how they voted in the election, too" (Vescey, 1980).[93]

The Moral Majority was politically effective because its members persuaded ministers to deputize a member of the congregation to organize registration drives at the church on Sunday morning.[94] The Religious Roundtable, on the other hand, functioned as a coordinating organization that brought together all the leaders of the New Right—pastors from many independent church networks, sympathetic congressmen, single-issue lobbies, and the electronic ministries—in one organization for education and political discussion.

The NCR formed a broad constituency that embraced the ideology of the New Right, combining economic libertarianism, social traditionalism, and militant anti-Communism. Economic libertarianism assumes that "left to itself economic interaction between rationally self-interested individuals in the market will spontaneously yield broad prosperity, social harmony, and all other manner of public and private good."[95] Government regulation of business and unions and government spending disturbs this harmony. Social traditionalism is concerned with "what is seen as the breakdown of family, community, religion, and traditional morality in American life."[96] The assumption is that the government has undermined the above by supporting such measures and movements as abortion, affirmative action, busing, sexual permissiveness, the Equal Rights Amendment, drugs, prohibitions on school prayer, and a secular course of study in the public schools.

The impact of the NCR was not long in coming. It was widely credited with being instrumental in the election of Ronald Reagan in 1980 through its activities, particularly its compilation and use of computerized voting lists. In 1984 it had an impact on the Republican National Convention and in particular on the Republican platform, which adopted almost all of its stands on prominent issues: favoring tuition tax credits for private schools, opposing the Equal Rights Amendment for women, making opposition to abortion a basis for judicial appointments, denying rights to homosexuals, eliminating laws against women working at home, passing strict laws against pornography, and instituting stern welfare policies. The NCR has also had a considerable impact on local elections. In 1988 candidates from the Christian right won two congressional seats in Iowa as well as six of twelve state legislative races that they contested. In Kansas, the Christian Coalition's candidate lost a race for congress, but Christian conservatives won eleven of twenty-two seats in the state legislature. Christian organizations contributed to the defeat of an equal rights amendment in Iowa and overturned gay rights laws in Colorado and in Tampa, Florida.[97]

More recently the NCR has suffered some legal and political defeats. The Christian Coalition's (an organization operating since 1989) tax-exempt status was revoked by the IRS in June 1999 because the IRS ruled that the Christian Coalition had engaged in political activity when it distributed voter guides in churches.[98] Furthermore, in the wake of the defeat of the attempt to impeach President Clinton and of the 2000 presidential election, religious conservatives have not been able to coalesce around a single candidate. Certain NCR leaders are urging the movement to withdraw from national politics and focus its efforts on "moral transformation . . . one person at a time, one family at a time, one community at a time."[99]

## Televangelism

The most dramatic development in the NCR's totalistic activism, consonant with its invasion of the political arena, is its invasion of the radio and electronic media. Such an incursion had long been constrained by the major radio broadcasting networks through their policy of giving free airtime ("sustaining time") to religious broadcasters as a matter of "public interest."[100] The major networks allowed mainstream national religious organizations (e.g., the National Council of Churches, the National Council of Catholic Men, and the Jewish Seminary of America) to sort out competing demands and select the limited number of speakers who could be heard on the restricted amount of airtime offered.[101] Only the Mutual Broadcasting System sold commercial time to religious denominations and that was limited. As a result, mainstream denominations dominated radio broadcasting in the 1930s and 1940s.

What destroyed the monopoly of the mainstream churches was the 1960 ruling of the Federal Communications Commission (FCC) declaring that the public interest was served by distinguishing between "commercial" and "sustaining" time. Station managers dropped programs airing free religious time and sold time to evangelicals and fundamentalists. By 1970 there were thirty-eight independent evangelical programs; by 1977 92 percent of all religious programming was commercial; by 1990, 75 percent of all religious broadcasting on radio and television was evangelical or fundamentalist.[102]

Fundamentalists and evangelicals have adapted quickly and remarkably well to television programming.[103] They have studied secular program formats, adapted them for their own purposes, and developed very successful television productions. Oral Roberts originally preached a sermon in the television studio direct to the camera against the background of a film showing him healing lines of sick and needy people in his tent meetings. Later he adopted the variety show format with "special guests" such as Anita Bryant, Jerry Lewis, and Jimmy Durante. This television program provided "bright contemporary music, attractive young people, a fast pace, superb technical quality, and a well-know presenter at its center."[104] Rex Humbard developed a glossy Nashville and country format with fourteen members of his extended family participating, and including gospel music interrupted by brief "sermonettes" or spots in which he prayed over prayer requests. Jim Bakker adopted the format of secular talk shows such as Johnny Carson and interviewed evangelical "stars" about the miracles in their lives.[105] Billy Graham has kept to the crusade format. Graham's crusade rallies in various parts of the world are filmed and later shown to television audiences. He has also produced "specials" that mirror rallies and include "well-rehearsed amateur choir(s) . . . local ministers or dignitaries read[ing] passages of scripture, [with] Graham preach[ing] a long sermon, and those who respond to his call . . . filmed coming forward for counseling."[106] And Pat Robertson has experimented with most of these formats as well as others including the magazine show and "Christian soap operas" to form the third largest cable television network by the early 1990s.[107]

What accounts for the astounding success of the fundamentalist and evangelical broadcasters in relation to their mainline competitors who have largely surrendered the airways to them? First, the drive to succeed was ingrained among fundamentalists and evangelical preachers, most of whom had to depend on their own charisma, hard work, and organizational skills to build up and sustain congregations. They could not depend on a relatively affluent congregation, as did the mainline preachers, to sustain them. They were also accustomed to the idea of measuring success by the number of followers they could draw and the amount of money they could attract on a week-to-week and month-to-month basis. That was the way they had always sustained their own families and congregations (i.e., fundamentalist and evangelical leaders were trained entrepreneurs who were used to selling themselves and their message).[108]

Furthermore, they had a simple and powerful message to transmit: the power of miracles, the authority of the scripture, and the necessity of being "born again." They were able to equate entrepreneurship in this world with saving souls in the next, and so raising money became an urgent task with transcendental consequences. This motivation made them much better at both winning followers and raising money than mainline religious leaders. Fundamentalists and evangelicals had none of the compunctions about preaching and raising money on television as many mainline religious leaders, who saw it as demeaning huckstering. In part this may be a result of the greater certainty fundamentalists demonstrate in conducting their affairs. Bruce has phrased this difference between mainline and fundamentalist and evangelical orientations as one of epistemology rather than doctrine.[109] Mainline liberal Protestants are relativists who "insist that we can only understand God's word in relation to our position in our societies and cultures."[110] That is, it is not possible just to read and immediately understand. One must interpret. Fundamentalists perceive scripture as authentic, transparently obvious, certain, and unchallengeable. Finally, messages propounded by "stars" are usually more effective than those propounded by groups, committees, or ordinary people. Televangelism continues the tradition of evangelism. The stars of the prayer meeting have been followed by the stars of the television screen: Billy Sunday, Oral Roberts, Bishop Fulton J. Sheen, Billy Graham, Jimmy Swaggart, and James Robison. The extent to which these performing stars also exert centralized control over the business operations of their ministries would also provide a competitive advantage over the more diffuse mainline leadership.

One might finally ask, why has televangelism emerged as a powerful force only in the United States? One obvious answer is that the religious culture of the United States has historically been evangelical, fundamentalist, and churchgoing whereas Europe's has not. Moreover, if one compares the organization of American and English broadcasting, for instance, one notices that English broadcasting is dominated by centralized "public" broadcasting with (up until recently) only four television channels, all public and without any sale of commercial time.[111] In the United States, on the other hand, the FCC has ruled that radio and television stations cannot restrict the amount of time sold to religious programmers. Indeed, it has proved profitable for stations to sell time to religious programmers, and they have seized on this opportunity to invade and dominate the television screen. Their effort is part of the fundamentalist drive to combat what they regard as the absence of religion on prime-time television, considering that 89 percent of the U.S. population claims a religious affiliation.[112]

This chapter's proliferation of examples of belief and practice from many different countries and across three religious traditions demonstrates the activist and totalistic character of confrontational fundamentalists. They have taken religion out of the worship center and into universities, markets, banks, homes, streets, and schools, as well as onto battlefields where they engage with fervor the established secular forces that they regard as dominating and corrupting their societies.

## Notes

1. All Quranic verses are cited from Abdullah Yusuf Ali, *The Glorious Kur'an*, Libyan Arab Republic: Call of Islam Society, 1973), unless otherwise indicated.

2. "Repair of the world" (*tikkun olam*) is an explicit goal in the ideology of Gush Emunim. See Lustick, *For the Land and the Lord*, 88ff. for details.

3. For a discussion of secularism among Muslims and its relation to other ideologies such as Islamic modernism, traditionalism, and radical Islam, see William Shepard, "Islam and Ideology: Towards a Typology," *International Journal of Middle East Studies* 19, no. 3 (August 1987): 307–36.

4. See Youssef M. Ibrahim, *New York Times*, 14 June 1990, for details.

5. Ibrahim, *New York Times*, 30 December 1991.

6. See Ari Goldman, *New York Times*, 11 November 1988, for details.

7. See John Darnton, *New York Times*, 3 March 1995, for details.

8. See Steve Weisman, *New York Times*, 17 June 1988, for details of the Pakistani situation.

9. See Steven Lee Myers, *New York Times*, 14 February 1993, for details.

10. See Clyde Haberman, *New York Times*, 9 September 1992, for details.

11. Ibid.

12. See Sabra Chartrand, *New York Times*, 12 November 1988, for details.

13. Ibid. Note that although many groups of ultraorthodox Jews (*haredim*), and fundamentalist Muslims and Christians seem to reject all aspects of secular

society, none of them do so. There are some aspects of a secular society they do accept (e.g., technology, many items of material culture, and some aspects of social culture). This matter will be examined at length in chapter six.

14. See Nadin Brozan, *New York Times*, 15 June 1987, for details.

15. See Gustav Niehbur, *New York Times*, 7 July 1995, for details.

16. See Ibrahim, *New York Times*, 12 February 1995, for details.

17. See John Kifner, *New York Times*, 26 July 1987, for details.

18. See Edward Gargan, *New York Times*, 17 February 1992, for details.

19. Ibid.

20. See Gargan, *New York Times*, 11 October 1991.

21. See James Markham, *New York Times*, 4 April 1989, for details of the Tunisian situation. It is interesting to note that in South Asia as well and with respect to religious nationalism of Buddhist origin, in the 1990s the secular government of the nation-state of Sri Lanka attempted to co-opt religious leaders and particularly religious symbols to assert its own legitimacy in the face of militant and violent opposition by religious nationalists. The government sponsored a kind of "state Buddhism" by establishing a Ministry of Buddhist Affairs, appointing Buddhist monks to government positions, giving them money, rebuilding the ancient Sri Lankan throne seat, and honoring the shrine that housed the Buddha's tooth, a sacred relic. See Juergensmeyer, *The New Cold War?*, 99–109 for details.

22. For a detailed anthropological analysis of the operation of "mosques of the people" and government mosques in upper Egypt, see Patrick Gaffney, *The Prophet's Pulpit: Islamic Preaching in Contemporary Egypt* (Berkeley: University of California Press, 1994).

23. See the anthropologist Patrick Gaffney's detailed and stimulating account, based on extended participation and observation, of militant and nonmilitant religious activity by fundamentalists and nonfundamentalists in southern Egypt in the 1970s: *The Prophet's Pulpit*, particularly 91–112.

24. See *New York Times*, 9 February 1992.

25. Gargan, *New York Times*, 11 October 1991.

26. See Ibrahim, *New York Times*, 3 February 1994, for details.

27. See reports in *New York Times*, 10 January 1980, for details.

28. *New York Times*, 28 June 1999.

29. See Ibrahim, *New York Times*, 14 January 1992, for details.

30. Ibrahim, *New York Times*, 26 December 1991.

31. Ibrahim, *New York Times*, 5 July 1992.

32. Ibrahim, *New York Times*, 12 March 1995.

33. Ibrahim, *New York Times*, 29 December 1991.

34. Ibid.

35. See Juergensmeyer, *The New Cold War?*, 50ff, for this line of argument.

36. Theologically, this belief shares certain elements with the Roman Catholic belief in the Assumption of Mary, who also did not die and returns from time to time to speak to certain of her followers or gives them signs. One of the signs the Hidden Imam has given to his followers is referred to as *qadamgah*, or "place of the foot." In various shrines or fountains what looks like a footprint is found in the rock. Many Shi'ah Muslims in Iran believe that the Hidden Imam descended to earth at this point.

37. See Armstrong, *The Battle for God*, xiii, 11, and 50.

38. See Armstrong, *The Battle for God*, 51 for details.

39. Ibid.

40. Ibid.

41. For Mary Hegland's argument about the reinterpretation of Shi'ah Islam in the year of the revolution from a passive religion focused on intercession and prayer to an activist religion focused on confrontation with the Shah's government, see Hegland, "Two Images of Husain: Accommodation and Revolution in an Iranian Village," in *Religion and Politics in Iran*, ed. Nikki Keddie (New Haven, Conn.: Yale University Press, 1983), and Hegland, "Ritual and Revolution in Iran," in *Political Anthropology* vol. 2, *Culture and Political Change*, ed. Myron Aronoff (New Brunswick, N.J.: Transaction Books, 1983).

42. See the articles cited above as well as Hegland's Ph.D. dissertation, "Imam Khomeini's Village: Recruitment to Revolution" (Ph.D. diss., State University of New York at Binghamton, 1986).

43. Armstrong, *The Battle for God*, 304. For descriptive accounts of the struggle between the Shah's secular forces and religious militants and other opposition forces during the Pahlevi period as well as the religious ideology of Shi'ah Islam and the organization of the Shi'ah *'ulema* (religious specialists) in the immediate prerevolutionary period, see Akhavi, *Religion and Politics in Contemporary Iran*, and Fischer, *Iran*.

44. Other religious symbolic acts of defiance occurred. On the first three nights of Muharram men rushed out into the streets of Teheran wearing white shrouds to indicate their readiness for martyrdom. See Armstrong, *The Battle for God*, 306.

45. See Armstrong, *The Battle for God*, 305.

46. Armstrong, *The Battle for God*, 307.

47. Ibid.

48. The concept of "Westoxification" or more literally *gharbzadegi*, "struck by the West" was popularized by Jalal al-e-Ahmad in his book, *Gharbzadegi: Struck by the West*, trans. John Green and Ahmed Alizadeh (Lexington: Mazda Publishers, 1982).

49. A popular cartoon widely disseminated in Iran during and after the revolution depicted Khomeini moving safely through what appeared to be a tidal wave (the Red Sea) while the Shah and Uncle Sam and their minions were being drowned.

50. See Alan Cowell, *New York Times*, 20 October 1994, for details.

51. See Ibrahim, *New York Times*, 8 November 1994, for details.

52. Ibid.

53. Ibid.

54. See Cowell, *New York Times*, 20 October 1994, and Ibrahim, *New York Times*, 8 November 1994, for details.

55. Cowell, *New York Times*, 20 October 1994.

56. Ibid.

57. See Haberman, *New York Times*, 13 November 1994, and 4 December 1994, and Kifner, *New York Times*, 15 March 1996, for details.

58. For a background discussion of martyrdom in Christianity and Islam, see Mahmoud Ayoub, "Martyrdom in Christianity and Islam," in *Religious Resurgence: Contemporary Cases in Islam, Christianity and Judaism*, ed. R. Antoun and M. Hegland (Syracuse, N.Y.: Syracuse University Press, 1987).

59. Joel Greenberg, *New York Times*, 25 January 1995.

60. As told to Greenberg, *New York Times*, 25 January 1995.

61. Ibid.

62. Ibid.

63. The following account is drawn from Neil MacFarquhar's report, *New York Times*, 18 March 1996.

64. Ibid.

65. Ibid.

66. Ibid.

67. Ibid.

68. See reports in *New York Times*, 26 February 1994, 27 February 1994, and 28 February 1994 for details.

69. See David Shipler, *New York Times*, 27 February 1994, for details.

70. See Alison Mitchell, *New York Times*, 26 February 1994, for details of Dr. Goldstein's life.

71. Mitchell, *New York Times*, 26 February 1994.

72. Ibid.

73. See Kifner, *New York Times*, 7 November 1990, for details.

74. Ibid.

75. See David Firestone, *New York Times*, 27 February 1994, for details.

76. Ibid.

77. Mitchell, *New York Times*, 26 February 1994.

78. See an excellent analysis of the covenant relationship between God, a people, and a land and its implications for three fundamentalist movements (in South Africa, Israel, and Ulster) by a historian: Akenson, *God's Peoples*.

79. See Mitchell, *New York Times*, 26 February 1994, for details.

80. See Imam Najm ad-din al-Ghaiti, "The Story of the Night Journey and the Ascension," in *A Reader on Islam*, ed. Arthur Jeffrey (the Hague: Mouton, 1962), 621–639 for an important traditional account of the Prophet's Night Journey and Ascent from Mecca to the sacred enclosure in Jerusalem, and from there to heaven.

81. For the significance of the biblical term Amalekites to Jewish fundamentalists in the contemporary world, see Lustick, *For the Land and the Lord*.

82. See Juergensmeyer, *The New Cold War?*, 153–54 ff. for details.

83. Juergensmeyer, *The New Cold War?*, 155.

84. However, many Muslim interpretations of jihad interpret it as the struggle of the self for righteousness rather than as holy war.

85. Juergensmeyer, *The New Cold War?*, 159.

86. Juergensmeyer, *The New Cold War?*, 160.

87. See James L. Guth, "The New Christian Right," in *The New Christian Right: Mobilization and Legitimation*, ed. Robert C. Liebman and Robert Wuthnow (Hawthorne, N.Y.: Aldine de Gruyter, 1983) for details.

88. See Philip E. Hammond, "Another Great Awakening?" in Liebman and Wuthnow, *The New Christian Right*.

89. William McLoughlin, "Revivals, Awakenings and Reform," as quoted in Liebman and Wuthnow, 221.

90. See Guth, "The New Christian Right," in Liebman and Wuthnow, for details.

91. Ibid.

92. As quoted in Guth, "The New Christian Right," in Liebman and Wuthnow, 37.

93. George Vescey, "Militant Television Preachers Try to Wield Fundamentalist Christians' Political Power," *New York Times*, 21 January 1980, as quoted in Liebman and Wuthnow, 37.

94. See Guth, "The New Christian Right," in Liebman and Wuthnow for details.

95. Jerome Himmelstein, "The New Right," in Liebman and Wuthnow, 15.

96. Himmelstein, "The New Right," in Liebman and Wuthnow, 15.

97. *New York Times*, 21 November 1992.

98. *New York Times*, 11 June 1999.

99. As quoted in *New York Times*, 7 March 1999.

100. The following discussion is largely based on Steve Bruce's *Pray TV: Televangelism in America* (London: Routledge, 1990), chapter two.

101. See Bruce, *Pray TV*, 26–27.

102. See Bruce, *Pray TV*, 30–31 for details.

103. "Fundamentalist" and "evangelical" are overlapping categories. Many Christian fundamentalists are evangelicals and vice versa. In this book fundamentalists are defined by the presence of particular attributes (e.g., protest against the modern world, concern for purity, activism and totalism, scripturalism, the practice of "traditioning," and selective modernization). Evangelicals are distinguished by their view that Christians must be "born again" (i.e., have a decisive religious experience as an adult that commits them to Jesus and to the religious life). Not all fundamentalists are evangelicals in this sense, and not all evangelicals share all the attributes of fundamentalism. For divergent views on the distinction, see Ammerman, *Bible Believers*, and Harding, *The Book of Jerry Falwell*.

104. Bruce, *Pray TV*, 35.

105. See Bruce, *Pray TV*, 39 for details.

106. Bruce, *Pray TV*, 34.

107. Bruce, *Pray TV*, 39.

108. See Bruce, *Pray TV*, 41–42.

109. See Bruce, *Pray TV*, 43 for the argument.

110. Bruce, *Pray TV*, 44.

111. See Bruce, *Pray TV*, 48–49ff.

112. In 1990 a team of scholars in communication, psychology, and psychiatry examined (through content analysis) one hundred fictional products on the ABC, CBS, NBC, and Fox TV networks and concluded: "the message being presented about religion by network television is that it is not very important because it is rarely a factor in the lives of the characters presented on TV or in the society in which they are portrayed." "Television characters almost never were shown attending worship or speaking about it." See the newspaper report in the *Binghamton Press*, Binghamton, New York, 4/11/92.

# SELECTIVE MODERNIZATION
# AND
# CONTROLLED ACCULTURATION

This book has argued that fundamentalism is an orientation toward the modern world with cognitive and emotional implications specifying outrage, fear, and protest against change, particularly against the ideology of modernism and the increasing secularization of society through the removal of religion and its spirit from public life: from schools, offices, workshops, universities, courts, and markets (see chapters one, two, and four).[1] Fundamentalists in many societies protest against the invasion of the mass media into formerly private domains, with cinemas within easy reach of every urban neighborhood and televisions in every home. In the United States the invasion of the corporate mentality into home and community as well as work life was documented by William H. Whyte in his classic, *The Organization Man*, many years ago.[2] Whyte also documented the rooting of transience in home and community as well as work life, with many of those who leave home for work life never returning to their home communities. A recent issue of the *New York Times Magazine* entitled "Business Class as a Way of Life," written almost fifty years after *The Organization Man*, emphasizes two things: the relentlessness of work for the American business traveler who can no longer leave it behind because of cell phones, laptops, and sky phones; and the simultaneous anonymity and homogeneity of a business traveler's life: all cities look alike, all airports look alike, all sounds are neutral (Muzak is piped in), and all spaces are bland (business sessions are now held in special rooms at airports, rooms that are comfortable, windowless, and decorated with video monitors). The essay on airports is entitled "Nowhere U.S.A."[3] Business people in the United States and elsewhere in the global society spend most of their time away from the individuals who mean the most to them: their spouses, their children, and their friends. "The number of hours Americans work each year has climbed skyward while working hours in most other industrial countries are falling."[4] The United States has replaced Japan as the number one country in hours worked, and Americans do not like it.[5]

From the fundamentalist perspective, modern life has not improved in the last half century. However, fundamentalists do not oppose all aspects of change; indeed, many changes are embraced and used to advantage. Fundamentalists support *selective modernization* and *controlled acculturation*. Selective modernization and controlled acculturation allow the acceptance of many technological and social organizational innovations introduced by the modern world.

Selective modernization is the process by which certain technological and social organizational innovations are accepted at the same time that other innovations are rejected. In this process, many aspects of the ideology modernism, which accompanies modernization (a basically economic process tied to economic growth) are totally rejected. Fundamentalists reject modernism; that is, the valuing of change over continuity, quantity over quality, and commercial efficiency (production and profit) over human sympathy for traditional values, even when they are forced to live lives defined by the modern world. Fundamentalists also protest many aspects of the life ushered in by the Great Western Transmutation, aspects fostering bureaucratization, globalization, the relativization of public values, and the pluralization of private beliefs.[6]

Controlled acculturation is the process by which an individual of one culture accepts a practice or belief from another but integrates that practice or belief within his or her own value system. One particularly appealing and effective version of controlled acculturation utilized by fundamentalists is antagonistic acculturation, the process by which an individual of one culture accepts new means from another without adopting the corresponding relevant goals; on the contrary, the new means are utilized to oppose the goals of the other culture, to undermine them, and to realize one's own goals.[7] Let us now examine several examples of selective modernization and controlled acculturation among fundamentalists in the three faiths.

## Modernization and Christian Television and Radio

Televangelism and Christian radio broadcasting in the United States illustrates these processes very well. Pat Robertson's Christian Broadcasting Network (CBN) has innovated in the fields of technology, organization of communications, education, and business. Robertson bought a defunct ultrahigh frequency (UHF) television station in Virginia Beach in 1961, "and with the money raised from preaching in Virginia churches, he put the station back on the air."[8] After experimenting with all kinds of program formats (see chapter five), Robertson proceeded to build the third largest cable network in the country. The CBN feeds into 5,500 cable systems, and provides an all-day channel of paid religious programming from other televangelists, entirely apart from CBN's own programming (e.g., the *700 Club*).[9] Using the money raised from the CBN, Robertson has organized courses in television and radio production techniques at "CBN University."[10] Using technology and business techniques developed in secular society, Robertson has borrowed, improved on, and turned them against both the internal and external enemies of his movement. The themes featured in his programming, of course, are very selective, featuring family shows, scriptural references, talk shows discussing religious conversions, and news shows focused on economic libertarianism and social traditionalism.

An even more interesting example of antagonistic acculturation is James Dobson's development of Christian radio. Dobson received his professional training in child development rather than religion—he has never headed a church. In California in the mid-1970s after writing a manual addressed to parents named *Dare to Discipline*, conducting medical research, and taking on a barrage of public speaking engagements that threatened to overwhelm him, he turned to radio and founded the program *Focus on the Family*.[11] *Focus on the Family* is a weekday half-hour program that combines religious wisdom with psychological discussion, merging discussions of guilt with discussions of God and Satan. Dobson soon found that the flood of 200,000 letters a month and 1,200 telephone calls daily inundated him, and again he was forced to innovate organizationally and technologically. The 10,000 letters a month that require special or emergency treatment—threats of suicide, fears of violence, and marital breakups—are referred to nineteen licensed family counselors who phone people immediately. The counselors have at their disposal "computerized lists of therapists and other sources of assistance throughout the nation" to which they can quickly refer.[12]

The 1,200 daily callers to the toll-free number, who are seeking further advice on the non-life-threatening but still important matters discussed on the program (such as eating disorders, learning disabilities, mid-life crisis, spouse beating, child abuse, workaholism, family finances, and sex education) receive more than fifty-two million pieces of literature and one million cassettes a year.[13] Mail that is less urgent goes to "60 staff members familiar with more than 1,000 prototype letters" on topics that begin with aging and run through the alphabet.[14] It is clear that Dobson has created a highly specialized, technologically sophisticated, and efficient bureaucracy composed of a staff of seven hundred people to meet the needs of his growing organization. And bureaucracy is nothing if not a product of the modern age!

Dobson also runs a daily fifteen-minute family news analysis program, a radio drama series for children, and a daily Spanish-language program, in addition to the half-hour program that is heard on 1,450 stations in the United States and overseas.[15] He publishes six magazines for different age groups and a political publication with 267,000 subscribers, telling them "what they can do to combat gay rights, abortion, and sexually suggestive advertising."[16] In 1988, Focus on the Family (the organization that originated with the television series) began organizing profamily coalitions in eighteen states. In November of that year, the organization sponsored the formation of the Family Research Council, a Washington-based research center directed by Gary Bauer, a domestic advisor to President Reagan.[17] It is clear that Dobson and his organization have modernized with a vengeance in the fields of mass media communications and bureaucratic organization while repudiating the values of the secular society that produced such innovations. With its myriad activities, Focus on the Family represents an activist, totalist, religiously inspired message that is also selectively modern.[18]

## Other Modes of Controlled Acculturation

Just as Christian fundamentalists were quick to take advantage of the opportunities and technologies made possible by the modern world such as cheaper UHF bands and the invention of the videotape (which they substituted for the more restrictive and expensive film) to spread their message to a variety of consumers, so too they rapidly accepted modern indices of success. The number of followers and the amount of money raised became indicators of the success of their various enterprises including their church congregations.[19] Fundamentalist church congregations boomed while mainline Protestant church congregations declined by the early 1970s, a trend that has continued to the turn of the century.[20] Christian fundamentalists were also quick to realize the power of organized numbers in the political arena, pioneering the establishment of the computerized voting list (of supporters) as the basis for a winning national-level electoral strategy. The use of such a list in the 1980 election of Ronald Reagan was widely credited with being partially responsible for his decisive victory. Christian right organizations have also used political parties and voting majorities very effectively in elections of state legislatures and local school boards.[21]

Acculturation has always been selective and controlled and is usually very effective at thwarting the opposition's goals and values. For instance in a rustic setting in downstate New York, a Christian pastor plans to develop a "Citivision Conference Center" and youth camp that will accommodate as many as seven hundred people for concerts, banquets, and fundraisers. It will also have a "Wild Wild West" fort, a chapel, heated dormitories, and a "Hoop Heaven" of National Basketball Association-sized basketball courts.[22] It is obvious that the pastor has selected aspects of the modern sports and entertainment worlds that will appeal to youth. But the modern means will be contained within a complex emphasizing fundamentalist religious goals through prayer groups, retreats, and chapel services. Moreover, the center will be used as a periodic gathering place for the four hundred pastors and churches affiliated with the Christian pastor's religious organization.[23]

Another dramatic example, this time of explicit antagonistic acculturation, involves the Baptist temple mentioned in an earlier chapter. The main body of the church contains a multimedia soundstage with appropriate lighting facilities; indeed, the church in some respects resembles a concert hall. One Sunday morning a nationally known popular singing trio was called on to sing a popular song melody with the lyrics rewritten to be a satire of religious pluralism. The featured phrases "Ecumenical Movement" and "Hindu, Muslim and Buddhist too, No! No! No!" were greeted with the most laughter. Everyone in the audience received the antiecumenical message delivered in an effective, modern, popular way.[24]

## Controlled Acculturation among Israeli Jews

An excellent example of controlled acculturation and selective modernization among Israeli Jews is the Responsa Project at Bar-Ilan University. For 1,500 years, Jews in the diaspora addressed questions to their learned rabbis living in many different countries. These questions were about the application of religious ethics and law to many novel situations in many different countries at many different times. The rabbis replied in writing, and these replies were collected in volumes known as the responsa literature. Using the IBM 3081 computer, the Bar-Ilan Responsa Project team at the university's Center for Computers and Jewish Heritage has put 248 major collections of responsa (including 47,000 questions and answers) into the data banks of one computer. "By asking the computer any combination of key words in Hebrew, a rabbi—or any researcher—can retrieve within minutes all the responsa precedents."[25] Instead of being confronted with "half a million unindexed questions and answers" and not being able to consult more than a few responsa collections, and those only after months of page-by-page searching, the rabbi can now immediately retrieve the relevant responsa.[26] Questions raised by new technology such as artificial insemination can be immediately addressed. For instance, a question regarding the permissibility of artificial insemination for married couples brought back an affirmative answer by one noted rabbi who stipulated, "provided the doctor was a 'reputed physician.'"[27] The Responsa Project is an example not only of controlled acculturation but also antagonistic acculturation. This fact is clear when one considers that—partly as a result of the project—the Israeli Parliament has ruled that Israeli lawyers can cite precedents from Jewish law as well as secular European codes when they decide cases in civil court.[28] By using technological advances developed in secular society, religious norms are now being applied in a secular legal arena from which they were previously barred.

The ultraorthodox Jews of Israel, referred to previously as the *haredim*, have gone beyond accepting new technology. Some have entered Bar-Ilan University, one of Israel's two largest universities, and registered in a three-year program in social work.[29] Bar-Ilan University is "a liberal, modern Orthodox institution, with a majority of secular students."[30] In light of the *haredim*'s avid pursuit of the strategy of separation (see chapters three and four) and their past avoidance of three major secular domains in modern Israel (the army, higher education, and the secular workforce), this entrance into the domain of modern secular education seems a radical departure. But the acculturation is controlled. The *haredim* (all male) rarely enter the Bar-Ilan campus, where they would necessarily have to go into an extremely affluent quarter and mix with immodestly dressed women. They take their classes in rented premises in Bnei Brak, an ultraorthodox and relatively poor city. Moreover, in a field (social work) dominated by women, by arrangement with the university they are taught only by men, thereby observing and preserving their religious norms of interpersonal relations.[31]

We have already discussed the American Lubavitcher *haredim*'s selective participation in Israeli politics (see chapters two, four, and five), traveling by plane to Israel to vote in parliamentary and ministerial elections while eschewing other aspects of politics.[32] Indeed, as Heilman has argued for the Israeli Belz *haredim*, "wherever ideology was silent . . . the ideological vacuum [was filled] with the up-to-date."[33] Heilman observed the Belz *haredim* traveling in the newest cars, purchasing the most modern video recorders, using the highest quality recording tape and the most up-to-date halogen lamps, and working on the latest personal computers.[34] The products of technological modernization were embraced wholeheartedly as long as they were framed and contained by the fundamentalist worldview and ethos and served its purposes.

## Controlled Acculturation and Selective Modernization among Muslims in the Middle East

Muslim fundamentalists pursue controlled acculturation and selective modernization in the domains of education, work, dress, mass media, and banking. Education has always been supported by the Muslim ethic and enshrined in such Traditions of the Prophet as "Seek learning [if need be] unto China."[35] Muslim fundamentalists follow several strategies in seeking education, but always within the limits of accepted interpretations of Muslim law and ethics. First, separate classes for boys and girls are maintained at the primary and secondary grades to fulfill the Muslim norms of modesty.[36] When that no longer becomes possible at the junior college and university level, coeducation is permitted provided protectors (chaperones or trusted third parties) are present. Even at the university level separation is encouraged where possible by televising or videotaping the teaching of male professors to an audience of female students in an entirely different classroom. Distance learning is avidly pursued in Saudi Arabia. When such physical separation is not possible, symbolic separation sets apart the genders through appropriate dress that marks the wearer as pious and different from the secular milieu that surrounds him or her.

Controlled acculturation and selective modernization are pursued adroitly in work and travel-to-work settings. In Egyptian television studios female production engineers wear the long gown (that covers the limbs and obscures the body's shape) and the Islamic kerchief that covers the head and hair (but not the face or neck). This mode of dress demonstrates their religious commitment and preserves their modesty and honor in the course of carrying out a job that requires much stooping and exposure of the body in awkward positions. At the same time, these engineers are pursuing a highly modernized occupation.[37]

In Jordan I became interested in the question of women's freedom to work and travel when I discovered in 1986 that many young women from the village of Kufr al-Ma had pursued a junior college education and were teaching in what seemed a haphazard spatial pattern in the surrounding villages of the district. This was an astonishing fact considering that when I began my research in 1959 no women left the village unless accompanied by adult males, and village education for women was limited to the third grade! How far, I wondered, would their families and the village community allow them to travel and work?

I was mystified by their dispersal throughout the district because although many taught in the village itself and in adjoining villages, others taught quite far away and seemingly beyond the range of protection and control. Then I discovered the key mechanism of controlled acculturation: it was the bus driver! The teacher would leave the village in the morning on a bus driven by a bus driver "of the peoples of Tibne." This was a phrase used by the people of Kufr al-Ma to identify persons originally descended from the mother village of Tibne more than a century before. In the late nineteenth century as political stability increased, the villagers of Tibne came down from their mountain fastness to cultivate and settle the surrounding villages of the district.[38] In subsequent years these descendants maintained ties through visits and intermarriages and all considered themselves related whether they could trace the tie or not. As such, they trusted one another to protect one another.

As long as the bus driver was of the peoples of Tibne, the teacher who left on the bus in the morning was regarded as well protected. The bus driver would make sure she got back on the bus at night and that no one harassed her on the trip back and forth. Because the bus often traveled quite far, a village teacher could work quite far away from the home village. On the other hand, other bus routes required a change of drivers (sometimes quite close to the village); that is, to a driver not of the peoples of Tibne (i.e., to a stranger). In these circumstances the residents of Kufr al-Ma would not allow their daughters to teach in the villages served by that bus route because they had no protection.

The concept of male protector has been applied to teaching even in such distant places as Saudi Arabia. Several village women have signed five-year contracts to teach in Saudi Arabia, something that would have been unthinkable in 1959. But it was quite all right as long as they were accompanied by a protector: a husband, a son, a father, a brother. The adjusted concept of male protector with its widening of appropriate roles (to include bus driver) and extension in space (to allow transnational migration for work) is a prime example of controlled acculturation and selective modernization.

Another example of these processes applied to the work milieu is the Jordanian practice of permitting coeducation in the process of getting a professional degree (e.g., in teaching or medicine), but insisting on gender-segregated work settings to practice the skills earned coeducationally. Thus a woman might be allowed to learn medicine in certain protected coeducational settings, but would then have to set up a medical practice in which she treated only women (and was thereby protected and honorable).

Islamic dress (al-zayy al-islami, as it is known in Egypt) is the foremost example of symbolic controlled acculturation. In the 1980s and 1990s Egyptian women generally wore three types of dress: folk, western, or Islamic. Although there are many exceptions, the first generally identified peasant women or women of rural origin in the city; the second typified upper-class and upper-middle-class metropolitan (Cairene or Alexandrian) women; and the third identified women who identified with Islam and claimed religious piety. The latter wore a long, flowing dress to the ankles with long wide sleeves, and a certain type of kerchief covering the hair and head (though women who claimed greater piety covered their neck and face as well).[39]

Although this women's dress was distinctively "pious," Egyptian university women also considered it moda, or fashionable (i.e., modern), again indicating controlled acculturation. In this case the same symbol is used to indicate at once piety and modernity. This dress, as did the women's Islamic dress in Iran (the *chador*, a one-piece head-to-toe cloak that could be adjusted to varying degrees of modesty and concealment depending on the situation), gave university women (and other women as well) a freedom and approval that they would not have received had they been wearing western dress in either the marketplace or on the university campus.

During this period men's dress in Egypt and in Iran also indicated controlled acculturation and selective modernization, but in a different way. Both Iranian and Egyptian urban men wore and today still wear western dress: pants; shirt with a collar, buttons, or cuffs or some combination thereof; and a jacket. But their facial tonsure (beard), or headdress (skullcap or turban), or both asserts their distinctiveness in nonreligious milieus such as markets, secular universities, factories, and business or government offices.

In the field of mass media many fundamentalist Muslims have selectively modernized with a vengeance. A *New York Times* reporter recently described visiting the media headquarters of the militant fundamentalist movement *Hezbollah* of Lebanon, a group noted for its military attacks on Israeli soldiers in South Lebanon. Today (at press time), however, it claims the largest single-party group in the Lebanese parliament, having successfully contested elections. It also has a network of hospitals, schools, and welfare centers.[40] But the crown jewel of its selective modernization is its information network. *Hezbollah's* information center in Beirut is equipped with mobile phones, computers, and a multiple-version Web site. Its television station, one of the most watched in Lebanon, issues bulletins on a regular basis, and *Hezbollah* guides provide videos to all visitors of its operational activities in South Lebanon.

This modernized communication system is, of course, completely controlled in the content of information provided: quotations of the Quran and statistics on weekly casualties inflicted on the enemy are juxtaposed with images of young, bearded "martyrs" and interviews with their widows.[41] *Hezbollah* uses the most modern media to disseminate its own fundamentalist message.

In the field of finance and commerce, Islamic banking is an excellent final example of controlled acculturation and selective modernization globally as well as in the Middle East. A number of Quranic verses (30:39; 4:160–61; 3:130; 2:275–76; and 278–80) have traditionally been regarded as prohibiting receiving interest (*riba*) and interpreted by Muslim scholars as usury.[42] In the 1950s and 1960s Islamic banks were established, but they operated only on the basis of profit and loss and contracts based on partnership and *commenda*, a particular form of trust allowing the transfer of goods. Both forms of contract have been approved by Muslim scholars,[43] but both were restrictive of banking practice and somewhat risky. The traditional scholarly view argued that Islamic law defined money as "coin," a medium of exchange only, and that money cannot be sold for money (i.e., charging an extra sum against time [the western concept of bank interest]).[44]

By the end of the twentieth century, many Muslim scholars had reinterpreted the concept of *riba* to regard it as a legal rather than economic concept, and by doing so allowed for fixed interest in certain kinds of contracts. Moreover, the concept of paying a "fine" is now accepted widely in Islamic banking as well as the concept of charging variable fees or commissions. Moreover, the traditional Muslim view that money must first be risked to earn a return has been reinterpreted to allow risk minimization in the form of many new kinds of short-term contracts.[45] All these reinterpretations have permitted the kind of flexibility that allows Muslims to participate in modern banking within the context of a Muslim value system. Today Islamic banks have assets of more than one hundred billion dollars, and Islamic banks or Islamic branches of conventional banks are found in most Muslim countries as well as in many western countries including Australia![46]

Although many Muslim fundamentalists reject these reinterpretations, others do not and have established Islamic banks based on the new interpretations. In this case modes of bureaucratic and financial as well as technological modernization are embraced in a creative manner (controlled acculturation is usually creative) at the same time that they are framed within the fundamentalist worldview and ethos (and thereby made authentic).

# Notes

1. See chapter one for the details of the argument.

2. See Whyte, *The Organization Man*, and the discussion by Arlie R. Hochschild and Virginia Postrel in *New York Times*, 17 January 1999 (published on the occasion of his death) of the significance of his book for social change in the United States in the last year of the century.

3. See "Business Class as a Way of Life," Special Issue, the *New York Times Magazine*, March 8, 1999, for details.

4. Greenhouse, *New York Times*, 5 September 1999.

5. Ibid.

6. See Lawrence, *Defenders of God*, for an excellent exposition of the argument.

7. See the excellent discussion of acculturation by the anthropologists Raymond Teske and Bardin Nelson in "Acculturation and Assimilation: A Clarification," *American Ethnologist* 1, no. 2 (May 1974). Although benefiting greatly from their discussion, I have departed from their usage in two respects. First, I regard acculturation as something accomplished by and characteristic of individuals and not accomplished by and characteristic of groups. Second, I view antagonistic acculturation as a subcategory of controlled acculturation, which I regard as the more general process.

8. See Bruce, *Pray TV*, 39 for details.

9. Ibid.

10. Ibid.

11. See the article by *New York Times* religion correspondent Peter Steinfels, 5 June 1990, for details.

12. Ibid.

13. Ibid.

14. Ibid.

15. Ibid.

16. Ibid.

17. Early in 1999 Bauer announced his candidacy for the Republican Party's nomination for president and began campaigning in Iowa and New Hampshire.

18. Dobson has denied all political ambitions, stating that "I have no qualification for political life" and "I will never be a candidate for public office." But his stands on political questions, his political magazine, and his employing Christian fundamentalists such as Bauer who do have pronounced political ambitions indicates that just as his psychology and religion merge, so do his politics and religion.

19. Pat Robertson, who formed the nonprofit CBN in 1960, has also built up a communications empire called "International Family Entertainment" that offers shares on the New York Stock Exchange. In 1992 his annual salary as chairman of International Family Entertainment was about $372,000. See the report "Evangelical Roots to Wall St. Riches," *New York Times*, 18 April 1992.

20. For a dramatic example of this trend, see the film *Protestant Spirit U.S.A*, which compares a mainline Methodist church with a fundamentalist Baptist temple in Indianapolis, Indiana, in the 1970s. Buses rolled into the Baptist temple grounds Sunday morning, delivering congregants from the surrounding area. The Baptist temple supported more than fifty separate but simultaneous Sunday school classes during the morning.

21. See Steve Bruce, *The Rise and Fall of the New Christian Right: Conservative Politics in America 1978–1988* (New York: Oxford University Press, 1988) and Robert C. Liebman and Robert Wuthnow, *The New Christian Right: Mobilization and Legitimation*, 1983 for details.

22. As reported by Claudia Howe, *New York Times*, 26 November 1998.

23. Ibid.

24. The Ecumenical Movement is sponsored by the mainline Protestant churches in the United States and aims to bring together for religious dialogue various Protestant sects as well as Roman Catholics and Greek Orthodox. The Ecumenical Movement also believes in dialogue with members of other religious traditions. Fundamentalists are generally opposed to such dialogue and regard it, to say the least, as the watering down of Christianity, and to say the most, as radical departure from it because it does not focus on scripture, does not insist on Jesus as a personal savior, and takes positions on social issues opposed to social traditionalism and economic libertarianism.

25. See article by *New York Times* correspondent Thomas Friedman, 24 November 1984, for details.

26. Ibid.

27. Ibid.

28. Ibid.

29. See Deborah Sontag's article in *New York Times*, 3 July 1999, for details.

30. Ibid.

31. Ibid.

32. The Lubavitcher *haredim* again traveled to Israel in large numbers in the summer of 1999 to vote in the Israeli national elections.

33. Heilman, *Defenders of the Faith*, 57.

34. Ibid.

35. See Antoun, *Muslim Preacher in the Modern World*, chapter five, for a description and analysis of Muslim norms regarding education as propagated by a Jordanian village preacher.

36. See Antoun, "On the Modesty of Women in Arab Muslim Villages: An Accommodation of Traditions," *American Anthropologist* 70 (August 1968) for a detailed description and analysis of the pattern of modesty.

37. See the documentary film *A Veiled Revolution*, produced by Elizabeth Fernea (New York, 1982), for examples of such women.

38. See Antoun, "On the Modesty of Women" for details.

39. See Andrea Rugh, *Reveal and Conceal: Dress in Contemporary Egypt* (Syracuse, N.Y.: Syracuse University Press, 1986) for a description of folk and Islamic dress in Egypt in the 1970s and early 1980s. See Fadwa El Guindi, "Veiling Infitah with Muslim Ethic: Egypt's Contemporary Islamic Movement," *Social Problems* 28 (February 1981) for a detailed analysis of the symbolic meanings of women's Islamic dress on university campuses in the same period. See also Arlene Macleod's important book, *Accommodating Protest: Working Women, the New Veiling and Change in Cairo* (New York: Columbia University Press, 1991) for a discussion of working class women's Islamic dress at a somewhat later period.

40. See John Burns, *New York Times*, 12 February 2000, for details.

41. Ibid.

42. See Gamal M. Badr, "Interest on Capital in Islamic Law," *American-Arab Affairs* 29 (Summer 1989) for details.

43. See Abdullah Saeed, *Islamic Banking and Interest: A Study of the Prohibition of Riba and Its Contemporary Interpretation* (Leiden, The Netherlands: E. J. Brill, 1996), for details.

44. Ibid.

45. Ibid.

46. Ibid.

# THE PROPHET'S WAY: CONVERSATIONS WITH A MUSLIM FUNDAMENTALIST

This chapter illustrates in a vivid and in-depth way many of fundamentalism's prominent themes—scripturalism, traditioning, activism, a concern for salvation and one's fate in the hereafter, orthopraxy, and the struggle between good and evil. It is a case study of one tradition, the Islamic, drawing on my own fieldwork in Jordan.

The account that follows records a set of spontaneous conversations between me and a number of Muslim fundamentalists. One in particular, whom I have named Omar, was trying to convert me to Islam in the Jordanian village of Kufr al-Ma in 1986. The conversations take place in Omar's pickup truck as we are driving together with his covillagers to attend evening prayer at Omar's mosque in the nearby market town. The conversations continue in the mosque with him, his covillagers, and other worshipers; during supper following the evening prayer; and the next morning after breakfast. This account will be followed by a brief analysis of the conversations and their significance for the themes pursued in this book.

## The Jordanian Context of Islamic Resurgence

To understand the significance of the conversations recorded below one must appreciate their context: a Jordanian rural society in which modes of learning had changed, traditions were being questioned, religious resurgence was well under way, and transnational migration had triggered economic and attitudinal change.[1]

Transnational migration for higher education and work increased rapidly after the OPEC oil-pricing revolution of 1973.[2] The rise in oil prices led the leading Arabian oil-producing countries to accelerate development schemes, which in turn led to increased demand for skilled and unskilled labor from outside Arabia, mainly from the Arab world and Europe. By 1986, seventy-two villagers from Kufr al-Ma had worked in Arabia in eight different countries in occupations that included the following: teachers, soldiers, health specialists, business managers, accountants, engineers, clerks, surveyors, translators, telephone operators, automobile mechanics, masons, construction workers, and drivers. All had stayed a year and most had stayed five years or more. One-fourth had stayed abroad between ten and eighteen years. Many had quadrupled the incomes they received in Jordan. More startling, thirty-six men had returned from study abroad and thirty-five were currently pursuing higher education in fourteen different countries including Pakistan, Egypt, Greece, Lebanon, Syria, Turkey, Romania, Yugoslavia, Russia, Germany, England, and the United States. Their studies ranged from engineering, medicine, agriculture, journalism, and law, to English literature, Arabic literature, and Islamic studies, and from political science to naval science, veterinary medicine, and linguistics. This in a village that in 1960 had a primary school for boys only up to the sixth grade and a girls' primary school up to the third grade!

The spread of transport, education, and communication proceeded together and had interdependent ramifying consequences. In 1965 there was one telephone in Kufr al-Ma located in one of the village shops. By 1986 more than thirty households had a telephone and there was a long waiting list for installation. By 1986 the village had doubled in size from 2,000 to 4,500. The time had long past when every resident knew the social background, even the nickname, of every other adult member of the community and felt free to chastise and punish any child misbehaving in public. In 1981 the village became a municipality under the supervision of a municipal council that had the power to levy taxes and apply for loans to improve the infrastructure of the village. Projects that were carried out by the municipality in the 1980s and 1990s included opening and widening of paved roads, extending electricity to the whole town, extending piped water to all houses, and building a health center and a middle school. Twenty-five years before, all houses were built of clay and stone (as opposed to cement today), the village roads were narrow lanes with rock outcrops, and trash (the mark of civilization) was nonexistent because no one could afford to purchase food in glass or plastic containers. Only one man in the village purchased a newspaper, so there was no paper!

All these changes led to a questioning of the norms of village life including the norms of tribalism, which required all disputes to be settled by elders in the nightly village guest house sessions rather than in state courts.[3] But because of the opening up of economic opportunities described above, the dominance of commuting (outside the village) for work, the electrification of the village, and the spread of television, only one active guest house remained available for the settlement of disputes by 1986, where there had been fifteen in 1960.

The process of religious learning (and learning in general) had changed radically since 1960 when learning took place in the home (either the teacher's or the student's) by a series of peripatetic religious teachers/preachers who spent a year or two in each village, teaching primary school age students the Quran, the Traditions of the Prophet, and other books they knew. When they would leave for another village, they would be replaced sporadically by another itinerant teacher/preacher.[4] Frequently the parents of the student provided the teacher/preacher with regular board and a sum of money on completion of the student's study (often the memorization of some portion of the Quran). By the 1980s this personalistic, multiplex, home-oriented mode of teaching was replaced by classes in state-run schoolrooms, and at the higher levels of education by the granting of degrees (which had been unknown in the previous mode of learning because the student's achievement was indexed by the number of books read, the prominence of the teacher, and the reputation of his scholarship).

These changes were accompanied by others in the field of religion. Religion in Jordan in the 1970s, 1980s, and 1990s was gradually bureaucratized.

All preachers in all mosques became government employees and received stipends from the state (formerly, the village preacher had been paid by the inhabitants of each village) not only for preaching but also for witnessing marriage contracts and serving as pilgrim guides to Mecca. In the 1970s the government established a two-year preaching college in the capital, Amman, and it trained preachers according to a set curriculum taught by state-appointed professors (rather than the previous freewheeling peripatetic teachers/preachers). The college granted certificates and degrees that qualified graduates for particular positions in the bureaucracy as preachers and teachers.[5] During this period the government also issued an edict stipulating the monitoring and chastisement of all preachers in local mosques for delivering "political" sermons.

Religious resurgence in the 1980s was marked by the intensification of worship and other religious activity, most of it outside the mosque. Many students from the village had attended or were attending religious universities in Saudi Arabia or junior colleges in the nearby regional capital, majoring in religious subjects such as Islamic law. Voluntary private associations such as a Quranic school (*dar al-quran*) and a charitable association supporting women's activities were formed in the village to advance religious values including learning and benevolence. Religious books were more widely available in the village as a result of religious philanthropic organizations located in neighboring Saudi Arabia, and religious book fairs took place frequently in the leading towns. Pilgrimages to Mecca from the village proliferated: performance of the *'umra*, the visitation of Mecca outside the main season of pilgrimage, which had been a rarity in the 1960s, was now common. Whereas there had been only a few elderly men who bore the title *hajji* ("pilgrim," a title of respect received for every Muslim making the pilgrimage to Mecca), by the 1980s there were many who bore the title, including relatively young men. The dress of men and women had also become markedly more religious with many men growing beards and wearing small white skullcaps and many women wearing modes of Islamic dress referred to in the last chapter.

All this activity was part of a general religious resurgence and a growth of fundamentalism. One of its aspects was increasing attempts by villagers, mainly young men—whether in the street, in grocery shops, or in homes—to convert me to Islam. I had been working in the village on and off for twenty-five years, and it was only in 1986 that this new religious ethos forcefully impressed itself on my consciousness. Omar's attempt described below was but one of many I encountered in the new era.

## The Fundamentalist and the Journey in the Truck

Omar is a picturesque middle-aged man with a long beard and a long, white Arabian gown from a neighboring village. I first met him by chance on the main road to Kufr al-Ma as he and a relative were repairing a truck. A few weeks later we met accidentally again, and he told me that next week he would come and take me to his mosque in town. He apparently had made inquiries about me and was told that I was an American interested in studying Islam. We were accompanied in the truck by four other males from Omar's village, one an intense bright-eyed man and his small son whom he had taken out of school for three days to go on a missionary circuit (*jawla*), or "going out" (*khuruj*), that was to take place in one of the villages of the district after the Friday congregational worship service.[6] Another was a fat square man who didn't say much but slept next to me in the courtyard of the mosque that evening, and the fourth was a bearded man wearing a Jordanian army red checkered shawl (*kafiyya*). The following is a reconstruction from my notes of our conversations.[7]

> *Omar:* Do you believe in the afterlife?
>
> *Antoun:* I'm not sure.
>
> *Omar:* Do you believe that Muhammad was the Messenger of God?
>
> *Antoun:* I believe he was a great man, wise.

Omar said that we were going to the mosque in town and we would sleep there overnight. I protested that I hadn't planned to stay in town overnight and that I didn't have my toothbrush. Omar ignored my protest and continued: "You'll see how everything is done in a Sunni [according to the tradition of the Prophet] fashion—eating, sleeping." He said that one had to save some time for the next world not (spend) everything for this world (*al-dunya*).

*Omar:* What party [*hizb*] are you from?[8] Are you a member of the Communist Party?

*Antoun:* No

*Omar:* "We don't believe in parties."

*Antoun:* "I thought there was God's party and the devil's party."

*Omar:* We all want to enter into God's compassion. Muhammad asked a Jew to recite the profession of faith.[9] He looked at his father; his father said, 'Do it,' and he did and the Prophet stroked his thighs and said, 'Praise be to God we have saved a soul from the fire [Hell].'

At this point in our journey the other villager sitting next to me in the cab of the truck lit up a cigarette.

*Omar:* "Smoking is forbidden."

*Villager:* "Where does it say that?"

*Omar:* "The Traditions of the Prophet. They forbid everything that harms the body. Besides, it [smoking] costs money; the taste in the mouth is bad—the wife complains. It leads to death [cancer]."

*Antoun:* "Garlic is stronger [than tobacco]."

*Omar:* The Prophet said 'He who eats garlic and onions shouldn't go to the mosque.' He paused. "If you disagree with something I say, say so. There is no constraint on you [to agree]." He continued his previous theme: "Smoking brings about a state of pleasure, delight, you're feeling well, [and that accounts for its persistence]."

*Antoun:* Smoking might help relieve tensions; otherwise the man might go home angry and beat his wife and children.

*Omar:* The Prophet said, 'Do not grow angry, do not grow angry, do not grow angry!' He said it three times. If you are still angry [after reciting the Prophet's formula], you are to perform ablutions [ritual washings]. If you're still angry after that, you should pray two bowings/prostrations [*rak'as*] and ask God for the anger to go away.[10] Before you perform these two acts, you should sit, if standing. If a person proceeds according to Islam his life will be all order, happiness, and security. When God created the person, he sent a catalogue like that for the car [i.e., the Quran] so that it [he] could keep working.

*Antoun:* "Where are we going?"

*Omar:* The Western Mosque near the fruit market .

*Antoun:* What group is associated with these activities?

*Omar:* "The group for [missionary] transmission [*jama'at al-tabligh*]; the missionary group [*jama'at al-da'wa*], that's what people call them.[11] But [the truth is that] the [whole] community of Muhammad [*ummat Muhammad*] is responsible for missionary activity [*da'wa*]."

He continued by noting that today there were many automobiles, much money, but this (material wealth) led to much anxiety. "It is all this world, this world, this world [*dunya, dunya, dunya*]! [As a result] his [the Muslim's] morals [*akhlaq*] are not good. [Pause] Are you circumcised?"[12]

*Antoun:* No.

*Omar:* The toothbrush [*miswak*] is made from Arak wood; brushing teeth with it is a tradition of the Prophet.

He took out his *miswak* and showed it to me.[13] He said that before a battle the Muslims remembered that they hadn't brushed their teeth, and they ran to the proper trees to get twigs for brushing. The unbelievers (*kuffar*) looking on said, "They are brushing their teeth to sharpen them so they can eat us," and they fled and the Muslims won the battle.[14]

*Omar:* If you depart in the way of God [on missionary activity] for three or ten days, you'll find out how the way of Islam really is.

## Conversations in the Western Mosque

Before we entered the small mosque on one of the side streets of the town, Omar told me not to take notes in the mosque.[15] Before we proceeded to hear the evening's religious lecture in the mosque, Omar brought a rather short, handsome, bearded man over to me for introduction. He started by speaking to me in rather good English—I discovered later that he was the evening's lecturer and probably some kind of leader. He told me that Islam had compassion for all men. That men had to be taught martyrdom. That the aim of their missionary activity (*tabligh*) was twofold: to strengthen Muslims themselves in their religion (i.e., its internal function), and the external function of spreading the good news (of Islam's message) to others (i.e., dealing with the outside, the non-Muslim world). I was then introduced to a Sri Lankan in the mathematics department at Yarmouk University, mainly, I gathered, because he could speak English. He told me he had been involved in missionary activity in Sri Lanka and had become involved in the activities in Jordan and had actually gone on a missionary tour (*jawla*) of three days in a village of the district where they read the Quran and visited people. Before he left the lecturer asked me if I could stay three days. I said "No, but I might come back on another Thursday or next week." He smiled and said, "Maybe next week you'll die first [and go to Hell]."

I noticed the proliferation of bearded men and the Saudi Arabian skullcaps, though many men didn't have such dress or appearance. Young men, middle-aged men, and older men were present, with both blue- and white-collar occupations represented. I also noticed or smelled perfumed beards and faces and one dyed beard.

The worship area was distinctive. The pulpit (*minbar*) was very low with only five steps. By way of explanation Omar said it was like the Prophet's pulpit (in Medina).[16] Only two wall hangings and two plaques, each saying "Muhammad" and "Allah" adorned the walls. Above the pulpit was written, "I have purposed withdrawal for meditation in this mosque as long as I am in it." The other Arabic writing was a Quranic verse on Mary and Zakariya introduced by the basmallah, saying, "Whenever Zakariya entered upon her in the prayer-niche [of the temple] he found in front of her nourishment." That is, Omar explained, God had provided Mary with fruits out of season, and when Zakariya asked her where they had come from, she replied, "God."[17]

The western mosque was small and intimate and divided into three sections: an inner worship area spread with colorful carpets and adorned with green furled posts; an extended prayer area with straw mats and rugs to the rear with shoe-stalls at the very back; and still farther to the rear in a separate room, an area with about twelve faucets for ritual ablutions with a narrow bench on one side and a small kitchen on the other.

## The Order of Events

The order of events that took place in the mosque for the approximately twelve hours of my stay there follows:

(1) Ritual ablutions (*wudu'*) in preparation for the sunset and evening prayers.

(2) The lecture or admonishment/warning (*wa'ath*) by the presumed leader.[18] The lecture was keyed to the themes of heaven and hell and judgment day. Humankind, literally, children of Adam (*beni adam*), had a choice between heaven and hell. The admonisher used the metaphor of the prince and the servant: if you married the latter you gained little; if you married the former you gained the kingdom (of God) as well as what pertains to it (the rewards of this world). The lecturer also talked about the Prophet's not getting angry at Abu Sufyan, his leading enemy among the Meccan Quraysh, saying, "He who gets angry, loses."

(3) A recruitment call for a missionary circuit of three days, ten days, or forty days with the lecturer urging people to sign up and not leave till they did. A bearded man with a red shawl recorded the names of those who volunteered. The admonisher said that all Muslims should visit others every day (their fellow Muslims, that is), those falling away from prayer or those returning from the Little Pilgrimage (*umra*) to increase (the strength of) social ties.

(4) The evening prayers occurred.

(5) The prayer congregation broke up into small circles inside the worship area; our circle was composed of Omar and his co-villagers. I was asked about my interest in Islam. I began describing my research in an Iranian village, referring to differences in economic status and religious ritual based on my stay in the two countries. Omar broke into my description with another admonition. I sensed that he feared that our conversation was becoming nonreligious in content and tone. He questioned me again about creation and the belief in the hereafter.

(6) Supper was served on a thin white plastic roll that was unfurled the length of the courtyard. Each setting was composed of a slice of bread alongside an orange and a cucumber set in paired opposites. We sat down cross-legged on the mats at very close quarters and were served four hot dishes that we ate collectively with pieces of bread (and without utensils) that we ripped up and dipped in each bowl. There was a salad bowl, a rice bowl, a meat and tomato bowl, and a potato-sauce bowl. While we were eating the villager with shining eyes sitting opposite told me that I must study Christianity, Islam, and Judaism and decide (among them). This remark was in response to my own statement that (despite my Christian background) I really hadn't studied Christianity and had probably studied Islam more. The villager asked rhetorically, "Will you lose anything (by studying)? And you might gain paradise." He said this very intently, leaning almost into my face.

(7) Sleeping pads were put into the courtyard where the ablutions took place, and small groups of twos and threes engaged in subdued conversation. As we were getting ready for sleeping, Omar showed me how the Prophet slept—resting on his right side with his head resting on his outstretched palm. And how the Prophet sat with one knee up while eating to prevent the development of a potbelly. He said that at mealtime the Prophet partook of one-third food, one-third drink, and one-third air (i.e., he always ate moderately and got up before taking his fill).

(8) I was awakened in the pitch dark with the starlit night over my head by the beautiful successive morning calls to prayer echoing from the town's mosques. I saw a few trees above the courtyard wall, followed by the sounds of worshippers performing ablutions: running water, sighs, moans, snorts, and preparation for entrance into another world, the world of worship.

(9) The morning prayer took place.

(10) A lesson (dars) followed the morning prayer.[19] The lesson was conducted by a short, stocky, bearded man whom I had not noticed before. The main theme pursued by the speaker was, "Your

future comes after death." This world was held to be of little account compared to the next. After the lesson there was another call for volunteers, and two individuals volunteered for missionary circuits.

(11) A period of meditation occurred. Many worshipers got up and left for home. But others stayed in the mosque to meditate, to read the Quran silently or aloud, or to form circles of villagers, neighbors, and friends for quiet socializing.

(12) Breakfast was served on the white plastic roll and prepared by Omar. Only about twelve to fourteen individuals were present. The breakfast consisted of eggs and salad.

## Morning Conversations: Good and Evil, Reward and Punishment

Following the morning lesson a young fellow in the mosque told me, explaining the verse on Mary and Zakariya that adorned the wall, that it (the nourishment) was God's reward to Mary for her piety because God rewards in heaven and on earth and punishes in the hereafter. And if a person departs from his religion, God punished him in hell and on earth. He recited a verse from the Quran (32:21) as evidence of his conclusion: "And indeed, We will make them taste the penalty of this (life) prior to the supreme penalty [in the next], in order that they may (repent and) return [to God]."[20]

This conversation led me to raise the question of the existence of evil. I asked in a number of different ways about the problem of God's creation of evil, the devil (al-shaytan). Omar's bearded covillager said that it was to test humankind. Someone told the young teacher from a village close to Kufr al-Ma who was speaking to me to "tell him the story of Adam." The teacher proceeded to tell the story:

The devil was a jinn who mixed with the angels and simulated their piety to the extent that he was called "The peacock of the angels." Then God created Adam and ordered the angels to bow down before him. The devil refused out of haughtiness since he was created out of fire whereas Adam was created out of clay. Thus was hostility created between humankind and the devil, and God put the devil [down] on Earth. God expelled him from the abode of angels for an intervening period to think things over—till the Day of Resurrection [of souls for God's judgment]. On judgment day he will go to hell along with those who don't accept Islam.

The teacher said that the devil had been created to test us; at the same time, God had given us knowledge and warned (us) against him. Another discussant said that God put Adam in the Garden with Eve and told him to eat anything except from one tree. The discussant continued, the devil said, "If you eat you will have a long life and wealth." Adam ate and God sent him down to Earth. Then Adam repented. God then warned Adam's progeny about following the devil. The discussant concluded, "God created good and evil and gave the person the reason/mind (*'aql*) to choose."

Two Egyptians had joined our conversational circle, one a knowledgeable laborer with a high school education, and the other a young man with shining eyes.[21] The latter now recited two formulas of religious piety: "I seek refuge with God from the accursed Satan," and " In the name of God the compassionate and the merciful."[22] Then he quoted a Quranic verse: "I have not created jinn and mankind except to serve Me" (51:56).[23] He ended by referring to God by one of his ninety-nine names: "God, the stupendous, has spoken the truth."[24] Omar's covillager punctuated the story and the Quranic verse, announcing, "We have given you the message; now we'll rescue you from the fire."

> *Egyptian:* When one of the companions of the Prophet was killed, he said [as he lay dying], 'I have gained victory along with the Lord of the Ka'ba.'[25] The infidel [*kafir*] standing alongside said, 'Your compatriot died—what is this victory [he's talking about]?' The other Muslim prisoners said, 'Oh that we could have taken his place [in order to attain paradise].'

> *Omar:* From the market town, 5 go out at once on a missionary circuit; from Amman, 15 [go out at a time]; from Pakistan, 150 go out (at a time).[26]

> *Teacher:* The Prophet said [in his farewell sermon during his last pilgrimage], 'I give you two [things]; if you take hold of them you will get a reward: the Book [Quran] and his [Muhammad's] Traditions.'

(As I noted above this was the dominant symbolism of the mosque with its *sunni* minbar, Quranic verses, and two plaques and hangings). Someone asked me about the state of religious piety (*din*) in Kufr al-Ma in 1960 when I first came to the village.

Antoun: They [the people] were religious.

A *chorus of others*: No! Not much. Villagers aren't religious.[27]

## Post-Mosque Reflections

As I left the mosque and returned to the village I noticed that no one mentioned during the entire set of conversations the American bombing attack on Libya, which had happened just a few days before, angering rural and urban Jordanians. Nor was any other overtly political matter mentioned, including the conflict between Israel and the Palestinians. And when I began talking about religious differences between Shi'a Iran and other Arab countries in the mosque the previous evening, Omar cut me off and proceeded to evangelize.

The next day when I described my experience in the mosque to the village preacher, Shaykh Luqman, and mentioned the *da'wa's* missionary circuits, he said that they called such circuits "going out in the path of God" (*khuruj fi sabil allah*); they go to the village mosques and stay three days and give a lesson after every prayer and go around the village and urge all to go to the mosque to pray. He said that they come to Kufr al-Ma once or twice a year during the summer vacation because many are schoolteachers. They sleep in the mosque, eat there, and study there. They say that they can't go in people's houses. That would be negating their statement of purpose, "We have come in the path of God," (and would also be sponging off people).[28]

A young villager from Kufr al-Ma who was taking a course of religious studies in a junior college in the nearby city and who had been proselytizing to me off and on during my stay in 1986 was not pleased with the fact that Omar had come and taken me to the western mosque in the city for the purpose of proselytizing. I never had the opportunity to ask him why he objected. Was it because he regarded himself as more knowledgeable than Omar with respect to religious matters because of his ongoing formal education and Omar's lack thereof? Was it because of Omar's

145

fundamentalist orientation with its scriptural stress on judgment day and the rewards and punishments that followed from it? Or was it for some other reason, for instance, the dislike of some *Sufis* (Islamic mystics) for the *da'wa*'s ethos, if not its worldview?

## Analysis of Fundamentalist Themes

A number of themes may be identified as running through the religious discourse in the truck and the western mosque: salvation and the afterlife, the struggle between good and evil, activism, martyrdom, scripturalism (in particular the Quran and Traditions of the Prophet), and orthopraxy.

The discourse in the truck begins with a question about belief in the afterlife and emphasizes that one's future (salvation) comes after death; this world is of little account compared to the next. The worshipers are concerned with the implications of action in this world for the next, spelled out in terms of Judgment Day and the punishment or reward that follows. This religious attitude is distinctively different than that uttered by the preacher in the local village mosque of Kufr al-Ma, citing a Tradition of the Prophet: "Work in the life of this world as if you will live forever and work for your salvation as if you will die tomorrow."[29]

A second theme running through the discourse in truck and mosque is the pervasiveness of the struggle between good and evil. This theme is raised in the initial reference to the "devil's party" and continues the following morning in references to the devil's place in creation in the discussion of theodicy:[30] the presence of evil is a product of the disobedience of God's commandments because of man's haughtiness and pride and the need to test humankind, who must exercise their God-given reason and choice and show repentance. The belief in the struggle between good and evil explains the ethos of urgency that underlies fundamentalist appeals and action.

After a statement that Islam has compassion for all men, the discourse in the mosque itself began with the evening preacher telling me that all men had to be taught martyrdom, and ended the next morning by one of the worshipers emphasizing the victory to be achieved through martyrdom (death). Martyrdom is the ultimate evidence of the activist orientation of fundamentalism—action to the point of death. The activist orientation of the worshipers was also attested to by the constant stress on the necessity to proselytize through "proceeding in the way of God" on the missionary circuit.

The written discourse in the mosque was dominated both by wall-hangings naming God and Muhammad and by a Quranic verse referring to Mary and one of God's righteous men, Zakariya. This verse became the focus of interpretation both by Omar and by a worshiper the following morning. Conversations in the mosque were punctuated by a recitation of Quranic verses or Traditions of the Prophet. And at the end, the teacher referred to the Prophet's farewell sermon, which again emphasized the Book (Quran) and the Traditions as the fount of religious guidance. Symbolically, then, the mosque was dominated by the Quran (verses, written and recited orally) and the Prophet's teaching, symbolized by the wall hangings and the distinctive Prophet's pulpit. Scripturalism reigned here. Directly implied by this scripturalism, however, is the didactic, orthoprax ethos of these teachings. This orthopraxy (focus on right action) was conveyed to me at many points through the late afternoon, evening, and following morning by many admonitions by worshipers about how I (and Muslims in general) should sit, eat, sleep, not smoke, practice personal hygiene, deal with anger, and behave in public.

The constant reference to Quranic verses and the Traditions of the Prophet also reflect the process of traditioning. These verses and traditions had direct relevance for the believer (and the unbeliever) in the present, and adherence to their injunctions would determine any person's eternal destiny: paradise or the fire.

Also important in the discourse is what is *not* mentioned. There was no mention of contemporary political matters either in the evening or the morning preaching or in the conversations with worshipers. This was so despite the dominant political tenor of Jordanian newspapers and radio broadcasts at the time (April 1986). They were filled with references to the hostilities between Palestinians and Israelis and to the very recent American bombing of Colonel Qaddafi's headquarters in Libya, an event that was universally condemned by the Jordanians to whom I spoke. This absence, itself, emphasizes the dominant fundamentalist worldview, which focuses on the importance of the next world, the struggle between good and evil in this one, and the role of martyrdom. The absence of such a contemporary political discourse also emphasizes that the threat to the worldwide Muslim community (*umma*) was construed to be less that of colonialism and neocolonialism in their overt political and military forms, but rather colonialism and neocolonialism in their more insidious cultural forms. This view demonstrates in turn the complexity of the fundamentalist tradition—which in its different modes and movements and at different times—that can be political or apolitical, confrontational or avoiding confrontation, separationist or integrationist with respect to particular domains of culture, and concerned with orthopraxy in this world and at the same time with one's fate in the hereafter.

## Notes

1. For details on the impact of transnational migration on villagers in Kufr al-Ma during the 1980s and 1990s, see Antoun, "Sojourners Abroad: Migration for Higher Education in a Post-Peasant Muslim Society," in *Islam, Globalization and Postmodernity*, ed. Akbar Ahmed and Hastings Donnan (London: Routledge, 1994), and Antoun, "Jordanian Migrants in Texas and Ohio: The Quest for Education in a Global Society," in *Arabs in America: Building a New Future*, ed. Michael Suleiman (Philadelphia: Temple University Press, 1999). For details on traditions being questioned, see Antoun, "Civil Society, Tribalism, Tribal Process and Change in Jordan: An Anthropological View," *International Journal of Middle East Studies*, 32 (2000): 442–463.

2. After the spectacular OPEC price increases of 1973, revenues of the exporting nations quintupled.

3. See Antoun, "Institutionalized Deconfrontation: A Case Study of Conflict Resolution among Tribal Peasants in Jordan," in *Conflict Resolution in the Arab World: Selected Essays*, ed. Paul Salem (Beirut, Lebanon: American University of Beirut, 1997), for a detailed description of the process of tribal conflict resolution of a case of divorce in a guest house of the village in 1960.

4. For a detailed description and analysis of how the old and new modes of religious learning took place in one village in rural Jordan, see Antoun, *Muslim Preacher in the Modern World*.

5. All public schools in Jordan at all levels including university are part of a state-controlled system.

6. Fundamentalists develop a special vocabulary to describe the processes and institutions that characterize their movement.

7. If quotes are used, the exact words are as I heard them; otherwise all conversations are paraphrases of the conversation based on my notes. In the dialogue that follows, material in brackets is intended as interpolation of what was said.

8. See chapter three for a discussion of the concept of *hizb* in the context of the process of traditioning.

9. The profession of faith is one of the five pillars of Islam. The believer must recite the formula, "There is no god but God, and Muhammad is the Messenger of God."

10. The five daily Muslim prayers are composed of a set number of ritual prostrations and recited ritual formulas. But additional prayer prostrations are religiously meritorious and may be performed at any time. Ritual ablutions are required before the performance of every prayer, but additional ablutions are also meritorious.

11. The Tablighi Jama'at is a Muslim movement of spiritual renewal founded about eighty years ago in British India. From there it spread to Europe and from there to North Africa. It has also spread to Malaysia, to sub-Saharan Africa, to North America, and as we see here, to Jordan. Barbara Metcalf, who has written at length on the Tablighis, quoted another source characterizing their activities: "The Tablighis . . . travel in groups on *gasht* (tour) to bring other Muslims round to their way of thinking. They . . . are non-political." She also emphasizes that they are distinguished by closely following the *sunna* of the Prophet and by their belief that "the duty to preach was incumbent on all Muslims." See Barbara Metcalf, "New Medinas: The Tablighi Jama'at in America and Europe," in *Making Muslim Space in North America and Europe* (Berkeley: University of California Press, 1996), 110–11. Most scholars, including Metcalf, do not regard them as fundamentalist because of their nonpolitical and quietist orientation. However, as we shall see below, they are fundamentalist in terms of many other attributes including their close adherence to a scripturalist (here the *sunna*) stance.

12. Although there is no mention of it in the Quran, Muslims regard circumcision of males as the index of membership into the Muslim community. Although Muslims should perform a seventh-day naming ceremony after the birth of the child (many families do not do so) to initiate Muslim identity, there is no stipulated time for circumcision, and it is not highly ritualized. Most families in the village circumcised their male children between the ages of three and seven.

Clearly, Omar attributed some importance to the ritual for religious identity.

13. The *miswak* is a short, thin piece of wood slivered at the end. At the main mosque of Amman, the capital of Jordan, *miswaks* are sold near the entrance, an index of its symbolic importance to many Jordanian Muslims of fundamentalist orientation.

14. It is interesting that the ancient Hebrews were required to perform strict rituals of purification before going into battle. The ritual purification of the teeth before battle seems to have the same rationale for Muslims in this instance. See Greenspoon, "The Warrior God, or God, the Divine Warrior," for the purification rites of the ancient Hebrews.

15. I didn't, and what follows is a reconstruction of the evening's events that I wrote the next morning.

16. In Medina a section of the Prophet's house constituted the first mosque for the Muslim community, and the worship space was very simple and rather Spartan, an atmosphere consciously simulated in this mosque.

17. Muslims recognize Mary as a revered figure. They believe in the virgin birth of Jesus. So important a figure is she for Muslims that one chapter of the Quran, "Maryam" is named after her. The verse referred to above indicates God's favor for her as indicated by his providing sustenance for the mother and child through his angels after the birth of Jesus. Zakariya, the father of John the Baptist, is reckoned in the Quran as being among the righteous along with John, Jesus, and Elias and as standing guard over the Virgin Mary in the prayer niche. The *basmala* is the phrase with which all chapters of the Quran begin, "In the name of God, the compassionate and the merciful."

18. One of the functions of the Muslim preacher's sermon is to admonish believers to reform their lives to gain the hereafter.

19. In Jordan, the daily prayers are often followed by a *dars*, a lesson with an ethical content either focused on the worship obligations of Muslims (prayer, fasting, pilgrimage) or on their interpersonal obligations (i.e., how to treat one's spouse, one's children, and one's neighbors). For a detailed description and analysis of the *dars* as it was practiced in Kufr al-Ma in the 1960s, see Antoun, "Themes and Symbols in the Religious Lesson: A Jordanian Case Study," *International Journal of Middle East Studies* 25 (1993): 607–624.

20. Phrases in parentheses are found in the original text; phrases in brackets are this author's additions for the purpose of making the meaning of the text clear.

21. Many Egyptian laborers and some teachers had come to work in Jordan as a result of the wave of Jordanian migrants who went to work on the Arabian peninsula, leaving shortages at both the blue-collar and white-collar levels.

22. These religious formulas are also politeness formulas that are uttered on

many appropriate occasions in everyday life. The latter formula, the *basmala*, is the phrase that begins almost all Quranic *surahs* (verses).

23. As quoted in A. J. Arberry's, *The Koran Interpreted* (New York: Macmillan, 1955). The jinn are airy or fiery bodies capable of appearing under different forms and performing heavy labors. They often appear as creatures of human form, personality, and intelligence, and in popular Muslim belief are thought to be capable of possessing human beings and controlling them for their own purposes.

24. Muslims, who are forbidden from depicting God visually (except in calligraphy), refer to him by any one of his ninety-nine names, each name referring to one of his qualities, "merciful, compassionate, all-hearing, all-seeing, and majestic," among others.

25. The Ka'ba is the sanctuary in Mecca that is the focus of the Muslim pilgrimage (*hajj*).

26. Indicating the greater strength of the Tablighi movement in Pakistan and its relative weakness in Jordan.

27. This answer is appropriate to the views of many urbanites that villagers are slackers in religion and that they are superstitious rather than religious. The answer is also appropriate to many fundamentalists' belief in the relative impiety of nonfundamentalists.

28. This behavior is notable in rural Jordan where the tribal ethic prevails and where people regularly give hospitality to strangers as a matter of course.

29. The Traditions of the Prophet (the doings and sayings of Muhammad) were gathered in two authoritative collections by the two Muslim scholars Al-Bukhari and Muslim in the ninth century. Each formal tradition (*hadith*) consisted of the text and the chain of transmission (i.e., the chain of narrators of the text going back to the Prophet himself). Thousands of traditions were reviewed (some say 300,000), with only those regarded as authentic being included in the collections of the two above-mentioned scholars; in fact, their collections were called "The Authentic" (*al-sahih*).

Traditions indicating different stances toward a particular issue are found, thereby explaining the ability of Muslims to take opposite positions on various questions as is evident here.

30. Theodicy is the vindication of the justice of God in permitting or ordaining natural or moral evil.

# CONCLUSION

Fundamentalism is one response to a larger transnational religious process that Danielle Hervieu-Leger has described as the "cultural disqualification of all traditions bearing a unified code of meaning, in a world committed to rapid change and extreme pluralization."[1] Global changes in communication, transportation, marketing systems, and social relations, along with the mass movement of peoples and information, have undermined the unified messages of all the world religions and their focus on a national and local hub of religious activity.[2] The response to this process has been diverse. The reaction includes a shift away from the pursuit of salvation in local religious congregations and attendance to "private religiosity oriented toward this-worldly realities and psychological fulfillment of the individual."[3] This can be termed a "do-it-yourself" approach to religion. It also includes the multiplication of transnational social networks that seem to be ever more influential, the latest instance being the Falun Gong movement that has spread across China to the western hemisphere.[4] A third reaction, and the subject of this book, has been fundamentalism, also a transnational phenomenon but of a particular kind. At the end of one century and the beginning of another, fundamentalism is flourishing, a fact that emphasizes the point that the decline of formal institutionalized religion does not mean the decline of religion in general.

Fundamentalism is a cognitive and affective orientation to the modern world focusing on protest and change. The fundamentalist's protest and outrage is against the ideology of modernism: the emphasis on change

153

over continuity, quantity over quality, and production and profit over sympathy for traditional values such as long-term interpersonal relations, visiting with neighbors and kin, nourishment of home and children, and the pertinence of the religious life over many domains. The fundamentalist's protest is also against the secular nation-state, which it regards as instrumental in pushing religion to the margins.

Fundamentalism's protest has arisen against the backdrop of a historical shift in power relations known as the Great Western Transmutation, which began in Europe at the end of the eighteenth century. Cognitively, the GWT undermined the organic worldview that had prevailed for centuries and that placed each class in its proper place for the length of the life cycle. It also kicked off a revolution of rising expectations as to what could be achieved on this earth in this life and led to the pluralization of private beliefs and the relativization of public values. That is, the consensus that had prevailed about what was proper belief or practice in the home, the local community, the workplace, and even the worship center has steadily declined. Politically, the GWT led to the steady reduction of "winners" and the proliferation of "losers" (i.e., both nations and individuals within nations became increasingly marginalized during the course of two hundred years). Thus, fundamentalism's roots have deep cognitive, historical, political, and economic reasons for being.

This book has emphasized that although the cultural content of fundamentalism and the specific historical circumstances that have led to fundamentalist movements have varied widely for Christianity, Islam, and Judaism, their overall orientation, their worldview and ethos, are similar. Islamic fundamentalism mobilized around issues related to western political colonialism during the first half of the twentieth century and to cultural and economic neocolonialism in the last half of the century. Jewish fundamentalism has mobilized around the issues of anti-Semitism early in the century and the Holocaust after World War II. And Christian fundamentalism in the United States has reacted to the dominant ideology of patriotic, progressive Protestantism and its preaching of the perfectibility of human beings on earth, as well as to the claims of positivist science as reflected in the "higher criticism of the Bible" and the doctrine of evolution.

But all these fundamentalist movements coalesce around and are defined by certain consuming themes: the quest for purity in an impure world, the search for authenticity in an increasingly pluralized world; the necessity for certainty (scripturalism) in a constantly changing world; totalism and activism in a world where the local has lost its coherence; selective modernization and controlled acculturation in a world in which secularization advances from all directions; and the centering of the mythic past in the present (traditioning) in a world where traditions are perceived as unraveling.

Because fundamentalism has been defined in terms of a particular worldview and ethos, it was appropriate to begin this book with a description of that worldview and ethos in terms of scripturalism and traditioning in chapters two and three, before discussing the strategies and practices that follow from this cognitive and affective orientation in chapters four, five, and six.

Scripturalism is a complex phenomenon. It is not defined simply by a literal belief in an inerrant scripture as most writers on the subject argue. Scripture is important for fundamentalists because of its numinous character; that is, scripture's capacity to bring the believer closer to the sacred simply by reading (sometimes just by touching) it;[5] its capacity to inspire the believer; and its emotional impact, whether in terms of comfort or transformation.

The fundamentalist's focus on scripture relates to his or her yearning for certainty in an age when, as one Protestant preacher said, "there are no fixed standards." Scripture also serves an important pragmatic, ethical function in all three fundamentalist traditions: proof-texts provide true believers with constant everyday guides for the conduct of their behavior in societies where the relativization of public values and the pluralization of private beliefs is widespread. Scripturalism also provides support for militant nationalism and justifies as righteous the use of violence (war) and self-sacrifice (martyrdom) for national purposes as the South African (Afrikaner), Israeli (*Gush Emunim*), and Palestinian (*Hamas*) cases demonstrate.

Finally, fundamentalists focus on scripture selectively, and often precisely because their enemies regard the verses cited as scandalous either because of their transgression of natural laws and processes (e.g., the Resurrection of Jesus, the Night Journey and Ascent of Muhammad, the Red Sea crossing of Moses) or because of their extreme character in terms of reward or punishment.

Traditioning reveals another aspect of the fundamentalist's worldview. Traditioning is the process of collapsing the primordial, the ancient, the heritage of the "golden age" with the present time (i.e., making them one and the same). Ancient events become immediately pertinent for daily life in the contemporary situation. Traditioning is the process of identifying with the good past and melding that past with the good present. Chapter three delved into this process with examinations of language, geography, food, and tithing among the *haredim* of Jerusalem, of proof-texts among the students at Bethany Baptist Academy in Illinois, of the biblical covenant and ritual among Afrikaners in South Africa, and of politics through the concept of *hizbi* (party man) among Jordanian villagers.

The fundamentalist's penchant for traditioning is underlain by the quest for cultural authenticity and by the belief in the struggle between good and evil against both the internal and external enemy.

Acting on the fundamentalist worldview and ethos and protesting against modernism and the increasing secularization of society to preserve one's own purity in an impure world can be done in terms of three strategies, either used exclusively or serially at different times and in different places: flight, separation, or confrontation with (defiance of) the established powers, political and religious. Chapter four examined the strategies of flight and separation in some detail, pointing out that both flight and separation can be physical, social (in institutions such as schools, churches, or political parties) or symbolic, or again some combination of the above at different times and in different places. Symbolic separation is perhaps the most interesting strategy, applied through dress, facial tonsure, demeanor, vocabulary (fundamentalist jargon), or rituals such as washing (ablutions), witnessing, or testifying.

The chapter on activism and totalism explored the strategy of confrontation in great detail with examples drawn from revolution in Iran; violent protest in Palestine; the battlefield in Egypt, Palestine, Israel, and Iran; civil war in Algeria; the resort to the ballot box in Turkey, Algeria, the United States, and Israel; the courts in the United States, Egypt, and Israel; televangelism in the United States; and banking in Pakistan. The chapter demonstrated that fundamentalists are not against change. On the contrary, they aim to take religion out of the worship center (church, mosque, synagogue) and into the home, the university, the parliament, the courts, the streets, the radio stations, the women's auxiliaries, the markets, and the battlefields.

A special aspect of the totalistic confrontational strategy that many fundamentalists pursue is the division of the religion of the people from the religion of the state. Fundamentalists rebuff the attempt of secular nation-states to co-opt religious personnel and religious institutions in state-sponsored settings (e.g., state worship centers, state television/radio broadcasts, and state pilgrim guides) by forming their own parallel institutions (mosques, radio stations, Web sites) and peopling them with their own followers.

Although fundamentalists generally regard secular developments of the last half century in such core arenas of activity as the home, the workplace, and the worship center with disdain (and often outrage), they do not reject all changes produced by the modern world.[6] On the contrary, fundamentalists embrace both social organizational and technological change on a selective basis, provided these changes (1) are consonant with their own values and (2) help them combat or cope with internal and external enemies.

Chapter six explored the great variety of contexts in which fundamentalists have innovated to reinforce their own values and goals: television and radio and the accompanying bureaucratic organization and mass-media money-raising to build their followings; computerized voting lists to achieve great advantage in political campaigns; computerized responsa to produce more evidence in courts; videos to give tours of movement battlefields; popular entertainment formats to hold the attention of followers in and out of worship centers; the development of surrogate protectors of women such as bus drivers to allow women to work in unusual settings and even transnationally; modes of modest dress including but not confined to veiling to allow women more freedom in school and work milieus; and special modes of "religious banking" to allow financial transactions in societies where religious codes ostensibly proscribe interest.

Finally, many of the themes presented in this book are given an everyday human face in chapter seven's short but in-depth case study of religious resurgence in Jordan, focusing on the conversations in truck and mosque between the author and a number of Jordanian fundamentalists. What emerges in these conversations is the focus on the Sunni way, on the "golden age" of Islam; that is, how the prophet Muhammad conducted his life in his own time—how he ate, slept, and controlled his anger. This emphasis on the Prophet's way is an excellent example of traditioning at work both inside the central religious arena (the mosque) and outside it (the truck).

Very prominent in the conversations was a focus on the struggle between good and evil and on rewards and punishments, particularly punishments for violating God's commandments. The worldview enunciated in these conversations definitely gave priority to life in the next world over the present one. In addition to the focus on the afterlife and the struggle between good and evil, the conversations in the mosque and the truck stressed activism and orthopraxy in a totalistic manner. It was not enough to have religious faith. True believers had to mold their lives on this earth to the religious standard in all their everyday detail. This standard required adherence to such everyday norms as those relating to eating, dressing, brushing teeth, and contending with anger. But this standard also required extra efforts such as enlisting in missionary campaigns and sometimes the ultimate sacrifice of martyrdom.

Scripturalism was a final theme given great prominence. The mosque's only artistic embellishments were scriptural in origin: the wall hangings with verses from the Quran, the name of God, and the name of the Prophet; and the low pulpit, symbolizing the Prophet's (modest) way. This was a way that had been codified for Muslims many centuries before in collections of the Prophet's sayings and doings (the *hadith*). After the Quran, the *hadith* are the sources on which Muslims draw most frequently for guidance and inspiration. The mosque itself was an architectural demonstration of scripture and tradition in the midst of contemporary life.

The fundamentalist adherence to scripturalism and the practice of traditioning have specific implications for how human beings relate their spiritual and worldly lives. Armstrong has expressed this as the relationship of what scholars refer to as *mythos* and *logos*.[7] Logos represents the "logical, discursive reasoning" we employ when we need to "get something done" and the "rational, pragmatic, and scientific thought that enabled men and women to function well in the world."[8] Myth is concerned with the "timeless and constant in our existence . . . the origins of life" and with meaning.[9] But a myth also "supplies the faithful with a way of looking at their society and developing their interior [spiritual] lives."[10]

The scriptures we have discussed are filled with successful myths, successful because they have lasted (been believed in) for ages. They include myths such as the various biblical covenants (Abrahamic, Mosaic, Davidic) uniting God with a people and a land, the resurrection of Jesus, the Night Journey and Ascent of Muhammad, and the disappearance and return of the Hidden Imam.

The anthropological view of myth applied here makes no theological judgment about the truth or falsity of particular myths. Myths are regarded as successful or unsuccessful depending on whether they are believed (or not) and made a basis of action.

Armstrong observes that fundamentalists often take myths literally as "a blueprint for action," rather than as "a way of looking at their society and developing their interior lives," as they did before the modern period.[11] This mixing up of logos and myth, Armstrong argues, can often lead to harmful and sometimes even tragic consequences such as Khomeini's endorsing the martyrdom of Iranian children during the Iran–Iraq war. This act led to the enlistment and death of thousands of adolescents, struck at Iran's demographic age and gender balance, and violated other equally powerful societal and religious norms such as the protection of children.[12] Witnessing through martyrdom is a powerful religious principle that is recognized in all the religious traditions discussed in this book (e.g., the Maccabees in Judaism, the Christians in the Roman fora), but it is not a practical policy for winning a war.

Finally, we may ask, why is it appropriate to describe Omar and his cohorts in the western mosque as fundamentalists when this term has achieved historical significance in a specifically American, Christian, Protestant context? Two caveats should be noted. First, neither Omar nor any of the individuals referred to in this book are fundamentalists, if what is meant by that term is that they reflect all the attributes and themes discussed. Fundamentalist is an ideal type. However, the lives of Omar, Hajj Muhammad, Pat Robertson, Dr. Baruch Goldstein, and the students at the Bethany Baptist Academy all demonstrate in various ways the beliefs, values, norms, and actions of a fundamentalist worldview, ethos, and way of life. Second, as this book has amply demonstrated, fundamentalism is a complex phenomenon. At various times, in various ways, in various places, in various phases it can be political/apolitical, confrontational/avoiding confrontation, separationist/integrationist, concerned with orthopraxy in this world/concerned with the individual's fate in the hereafter, or concerned with the external enemy/concerned with the internal enemy.

This book argues that fundamentalism is an orientation toward the modern world: a selective activist rebellion against that world and the reduction of the divine presence in it. Fundamentalism is keyed to cultural rather than political or economic images (e.g., bikinis, English/French television, foreign-language schools and law codes, crime, high divorce rates, pornography, drug abuse, appropriate dress and demeanor). Fundamentalists are disturbed by the impact of modern technology (rather than the technology itself), transport, and communication systems on the intimate, personalistic networks that characterized peasant and tribal societies in the preindustrial period; these networks have often been rended by modernization.

Although fundamentalism is sometimes apolitical in its orientation to contemporary political contests at either the national or the local level, it has been shaped by a shifting power balance in which Third World citizens have become increasingly disadvantaged with the steady reduction in the number of world powers. It has been shaped by an environment in which an increasing number of people in the First, Second, and Third Worlds find themselves unable to share the benefits of an increasingly consumer society. In these terms, the adherence to scripture or its constant citation, although an attribute of fundamentalism and central to its symbolism and form, is not its defining characteristic; nor, for that matter, is it defined by the otherworldly orientation that is often so prominent in its discourse. Rather, fundamentalism is an orientation to the modern world that is inherently oppositional and minoritarian (the outs protesting against the ins); determinedly activist (in its determination to change the status quo whether through confrontation or separation), and in that sense not otherworldly at all; decidedly Manichean in its description of the struggle between good and evil in the contemporary world;[13] and innovative in its willingness to use various tactics in various milieus (and not therefore "traditional"). Such tactics include computerized voting lists; formal political parties; street demonstrations; informal networks; letter-writing campaigns; videos and audiotapes; fasting; marching in religious processions; and gathering for collective action in cemeteries, schools, banks, hospitals, factories, battlegrounds, and *husayniyyahs*.[14]

Fundamentalism is keyed to opposing the cultural manifestations of modernity—western dress, films, dating patterns, language use, abolition of the gender-based division of labor, and weakening of family norms—because it is dedicated to maintaining a state of purity in the midst of the modern world. In this sense there is much in common among Jerry Falwell, Pat Robertson, Ayatollah Khomeini, and Rabbi Meir Kahane, and among the *haredim* (retreating behind their quarter gates in Jerusalem on the Sabbath), the Society of Excommunication and Flight in Egypt, and the students and teachers at Bob Jones University in South Carolina.

## Notes

1. Hervieu-Leger, "Faces of Catholic Transnationalism," 106.

2. Hervieu-Leger has pointed out that "parish civilization" is in decline. That is, the time when every inhabitant of a small (usually but not invariably peasant) community was a member of a local religious congregation with a familiar cycle of worship and feast days, and a focus on the local parish leader, has gone. Although Hervieu-Leger's formulation describes only the situation of French Catholicism, it is generally applicable to the case of Muslim and Jewish congregations as well, particularly in the latter half of the twentieth century.

3. Hervieu-Leger, "Faces of Catholic Transnationalism," 110.

4. For news of the flourishing Falun Gong movement in New York City, see *New York Times*, 29 October 1999. For news of the movement's principles and its recent repression in China, see *New York Times*, 31 January 1999, 22 July 1999, 23 July 1999, 27 July 1999, 30 July 1999, and 27 December 1999.

5. The religious traditions of Judaism and Islam surround the Torah and the Quran with norms and taboos regarding the conditions under which each can be read or handled because of their holy character.

6. This fact prevents them from being classified as "traditionalists," as, for instance, would be appropriate for a group such as the Amish of Lancaster County, Pennsylvania, who have rejected much of the technology of the modern age including automobiles, tractors, and (until recently) telephones.

7. See Armstrong, *The Battle for God*, particularly pages xiii-xv, 11, and 50–51 for details.

8. Armstrong, *The Battle for God*, xiv-xv.

9. Armstrong, *The Battle for God*, xiii.

10. Armstrong, *The Battle for God*, 51.

11. Ibid.

12. See Armstrong, *The Battle for God*, 327–28 for the argument.

13. Originally, Manichean referred to a believer in the doctrines of Mani, a Persian of the third century C. E. who taught a dualism derived from Zoroastrianism, specifically, that man's body is the product of the kingdom of darkness, but that his soul springs from the kingdom of light. More generally and contemporaneously, the term refers to beliefs rooted in the struggle between good and evil.

14. The religious mourning (for the martyr Husayn) halls in which the participants in the Iranian revolution often mobilized.

*ablutions.* The ritual purifications (by water) required for Muslims before prayer and other worship obligations.

*acculturation.* The process of taking on cultural traits without a change in the basic values of the borrowing individual.

> *antagonistic*—the process of taking on a cultural trait for the purpose of using it against the borrowed (alien) culture.
>
> *controlled*—the process of taking on a culture trait in such a way as to accommodate one's own values rather than the values of the alien culture.

*affective.* Relating to the emotions.

*agnostic.* One who believes that neither the nature nor the existence of God nor the ultimate character of the universe is knowable.

*atheist.* One who denies the existence of a God or Supreme Being.

*ayatollah.* Term derived from the Arabic, meaning, literally, "sign of God"; an honorific title for a leading Shi'a Muslim scholar in Iran.

*cognitive.* Relating to thought processes.

*deviation amplification.* The psychological process by which negative information is processed by the mind so as to appear positive.

*ethos.* The emotional tone, character, and quality of a people's life, its moral and aesthetic style and mood.

*evangelical.* Relating to a religious perspective that regards the Bible as a final authority, places great importance on spreading the message of salvation, and, above all, requires that all true believers be "born again" (i.e., "saved" [as an adult] through a personal relationship with Jesus Christ).

*gharbzadegi.* Persian term meaning "struck" (or contaminated) by the West.

*Gush Emunim.* Hebrew term meaning, literally, "Bloc of the Faithful"; both a fundamentalist and Zionist movement founded by both religious and secular Jews that practices militant tactics to promote settlement in what it regards as *eretz israel* (the land of Israel), the territory that was occupied by Israel after the war of June 1967.

*hadith.* (Arabic) Tradition of the Prophet; the *hadith* are documented accounts of the sayings and doings of Muhammad that do not appear in the Quran, but that were recorded by close companions and family members. After the Quran, they are the most important source of Islamic law and ethics.

*hajj.* (Arabic) A title of honor signifying the person who has made the pilgrimage to Mecca; also signifies the pilgrimage process itself.

*Hidden Imam.* The last of the Shi'ah Imams, who disappeared in the tenth century and is believed to return to earth from time to time to speak to certain of the faithful.

*Husayn, Imam.* Grandson of the Prophet and Shi'ah Muslim leader martyred at the battle of Kerbala (Iraq) in the seventh century; in Iran a religious cult is focused on his figure during the Muslim month of Muharram.

*husayniyyah.* (Arabic, Persian) Ritual mourning hall for Husayn where Shi'ah Muslims gather during the month of Muharram to mourn for Husayn; the *husayniyyah* is found in every Shi'ah community of any size including villages in Iran, Iraq, and Lebanon; the hall is also used for lectures and rallies with a religiopolitical content, particularly on matters connected to social justice.

*ideal type.* Social scientific term used to indicate a constructed role, position, or type with all attributes present and assuming that the type rarely exists in real life (e.g., as an ideal type the Mcintosh apple is large, red, juicy, and wormless).

*ideology.* An action-oriented system of beliefs capable of explaining the world, justifying decisions, identifying alternatives, and creating an all-embracing sense of social solidarity.

*imam.* (Arabic) Literally, "leader." In mainstream Islam, a prayer leader; in Shi'ah Islam, a direct male descendant of the prophet Muhammad who enshrines divine wisdom and who alone is an infallible guide to believers; there were twelve such guides among the Shi'ah of Iran.

*instrumental.* Referring to human acts keyed to achieving specific rewards for the individual.

*jahiliyyah.* (Arabic) Literally, "Age of Ignorance"; the pre-Islamic period in Arabia; Muslim fundamentalists apply the term to any society, including contemporary Muslim societies, that has turned its back on God by extensive violations of Muslim law and ethics regardless of whether the society is meeting formal worship obligations.

*jihad.* (Arabic) Literally, "struggle"; for Muslims the struggle to reform the self or one's community; more specifically, a war waged in the service of religion.

*jinn.* (Arabic) Spiritual beings of human form and personality mentioned in the Quran who have the power to possess humans.

*laymen.* Members of religious congregations who are not clergy.

*logos.* (Greek) Literally, "Word"; more generally, rational, logical, or scientific discourse.

*Manichean.* Believer in the doctrine of Mani, a Persian of the third century who taught a doctrine derived from Zoroastrianism, namely that man's body is a product of the Kingdom of Darkness but his soul springs from the Kingdom of Light; referring to the struggle between good and evil.

*martyr.* Person who prefers death to giving up religious principles.

*millennialism.* Belief, based on scripture, in the thousand-year period of peace and justice that fundamentalist Christians emphasize will come into being at the end of human history; this period will be followed by the Last Judgment.

*modernism.* An ideology produced by and at the same time encouraging the process of modernization. Modernism emphasizes individualism and values emphasizing change over continuity; quantity over quality; and efficient production, power, and profit over sympathy for traditional values and roles.

*modernization.* The technological and social organizational processes that lead to economic growth.

*multiplex.* Refers to social relations and roles that cut across many interests—economic, political, recreational, religious, kinship—and in so doing affect and change all relations in the direction of greater intimacy and morality (e.g., in many societies the father of the family is also a mediator, prayer leader, and cultivator).

*nation-state.* A sovereign state exercising authority within a certain geographical area and animated by the ideology of nationalism; that is, the belief that one's primary loyalty is to a national community and its distinctive political culture (flag, institutions, values).

*norm.* A statement that can be elicited from an informant as to what behavior "ought" to be in any particular situation in relation to any particular person or group; normative pertains to expected and approved behavior.

*noumenal/numinous.* That which is apprehended by the understanding rather than the senses; that which is the ground of things and in that sense unknowable and therefore mysterious.

*orthodoxy.* Right belief.

*orthopraxy.* Right practice.

*phenomenal.* Pertaining to that which can be apprehended by the senses.

*pillars of Islam.* The five acts required of all Muslims: daily prayer, fasting the month of Ramadan, pilgrimage to Mecca, the giving of alms, and the profession of faith. ("There is no god but God, and Muhammad is his Messenger.")

*pluralization of private belief.* State of modern society in which—at the community level—one cannot expect others to have similar beliefs and attitudes as oneself.

*positivist science.* Science based strictly on the experimental method and accentuating systematic observation and recording.

*Ramadan.* Muslim month of fasting.

*relativistic.* A perspective that when applied to society regards each society or culture worthy in its own terms and not subject to moral or ethical judgment in comparison with others.

*relativization of public value.* State of modern society by which no absolute standards are defended by public institutions (i.e., a "live and let live" attitude).

*religious resurgence.* Rising importance and visibility of religion; increased impact of religion on political life.

*secular.* Nonreligious; temporal; based on nonreligious ideology.

*secularization.* The trend of decreasing relevance and visibility of religious leaders, organizations, activities, beliefs, structures, and publications.

*shaytan.* (Arabic) The devil.

*Shi'ah Islam.* A minority form of Islam that, like the majority form, Sunni Islam, follows the five pillars of the faith; Shi'ah Muslims differ from Sunnis on which descendant of the Prophet should lead the community on earth; Shi'ah Muslims of Iran, Iraq, and Lebanon also differ in some of their key rituals and beliefs regarding the divinely inspired power of their leaders, the imams.

*sunnah.* (Arabic) Literally, "custom"; the habits and practices of the prophet Muhammad, recorded for posterity by his family and companions as the guide for the community's behavior.

*Sunni Islam.* The majority form of Islam, which bases its ethics and law on the *sunnah* of the prophet Muhammad; they do not require the Muslim community to be led by a descendant of the Prophet; collectively, they are called Sunnis or Sunni Muslims.

*theological.* Relating to the science of the existence and character of God and God's laws; systematic (and in that sense rational) thinking on the subject.

*tribal.* Relating to a category of people who claim extended kin ties, often of a lineal kind, often with a distinctive culture and political functions such as conflict resolution.

*'ulema.* (Arabic) Literally, "learned men"; in Islam the influential guardians of religious and legal traditions.

*ummah.* The worldwide Muslim community.

*universalistic.* A perspective that judges all things by a single worldwide standard.

*value.* That which is desirable at a basic level of understanding; a society's values are often not explicitly recognized, although the norms deriving from them are (e.g., not all Americans would recognize individualism as a value, but they would recognize the right to free speech).

*worldview.* The picture people hold of the way things are; their concepts of nature, self, and society; their most comprehensive ideas of order.

# Suggestions
## for Further Reading

## General

Akenson, Donald. *God's Peoples: Covenant and Land in South Africa, Israel, and Ulster.* Ithaca, N.Y.: Cornell University Press, 1992.

Armstrong, Karen. *The Battle for God.* New York: Alfred A. Knopf, 2000.

Bendroth, Margaret. *Fundamentalism and Gender, 1875 to the Present.* New Haven, Conn.: Yale University Press, 1993.

Brink, Judy, and Joan Mencher. *Gender and Religious Fundamentalism Cross-Culturally.* London: Routledge, 1997.

Juergensmeyer, Mark. *The New Cold War? Religious Nationalism Confronts the Secular State.* Berkeley: University of California Press, 1993.

Kepel, Gilles. *The Revenge of God: The Resurgence of Islam, Christianity, and Judaism in the Modern World.* University Park, Penn.: Pennsylvania State University Press, 1994.

Larson, Gerald. *India's Agony over Religion.* Albany, N.Y.: State University of New York Press, 1995.

Lawrence, Bruce. *Defenders of God: The Fundamentalist Revolt against the Modern Age.* San Francisco: Harper and Row, 1989.

Marty, Martin, and R. Scott Appleby, eds. *Fundamentalisms Observed.* Chicago: University of Chicago Press, 1991.

———. *The Glory and the Power: The Fundamentalist Challenge to the Modern Age.* Boston: Beacon Press, 1992.

———. *Fundamentalisms and the State: Remaking Polities, Economies, and Militance.* Chicago: University of Chicago Press, 1993.

———. *Accounting for Fundamentalisms: The Dynamic Character of Movements*. Chicago: University of Chicago Press, 1994.

———. *Fundamentalisms Comprehended*. Chicago: University of Chicago Press, 1995.

Oberoi, Harjat. *The Construction of Religious Boundaries: Culture, Identity and Diversity in the Sikh Tradition*. New York: Oxford University Press, 1994.

Riesebrodt, Martin. *Pious Passion: The Emergence of Modern Fundamentalism in the United States and Iran*. Berkeley: University of California Press, 1990.

Rudolph, Susanne, and James Piscatori, eds. *Transnational Religion and Fading States*. Boulder: Westview, 1997.

Tibi, Bassam. *The Challenge of Fundamentalism: Political Islam and the New World Disorder*. Berkeley: University of California Press, 1998.

Van der Meer, Peter. *Religious Nationalism: Hindus and Muslims in India*. Berkeley: University of California Press, 1994.

## Christian Fundamentalism

Akenson, Donald H. *God's Peoples: Covenant and Land in South Africa, Israel, and Ulster*. Ithaca, N.Y.: Cornell University Press, 1992.

Ammerman, Nancy. *Bible Believers: Fundamentalists in the Modern World*. Piscataway, N.J.: Rutgers University Press, 1987.

———. "North American Protestant Fundamentalism." In *Fundamentalisms Observed*, edited by Marty and Appleby. Chicago: University of Chicago Press, 1991.

Beale, David O. *In Pursuit of Purity: American Fundamentalism since 1850*. Greenville, S.C.: Unusual Publications, 1986.

Bendroth, Margaret L. *Fundamentalism and Gender, 1875 to the Present*. New Haven, Conn.: Yale University Press, 1993.

Bruce, Steve. *The Rise and Fall of the New Christian Right: Conservative Protestant Politics in America 1978–1988*. New York: Oxford University Press, 1988.

———. *Pray TV: Televangelism in America*. London: Routledge, 1990.

Carpenter, Joel A., ed. *Fundamentalist versus Modernist: The Debates between John Roach Stanton and Charles Francis Potter*. New York: Garland Publishing Company, 1988.

———. *The Fundamentalist-Modernist Conflict: Opposing Views on Three Major Issues*. New York: Garland Publishing Company, 1988.

————. *The Premillennial Second Coming: Two Early Champions.* New York: Garland Publishing Company, 1988.

————. *William Jennings Bryan on Orthodoxy, Modernism, and Evolution.* New York: Garland Publishing Company, 1988.

Dobson, James. *Dare to Discipline.* Wheaton, Ill.: Tyndale, 1970.

Falwell, Jerry. *Listen America!* Garden City, N.Y.: Doubleday, 1980.

Harding, Susan. *The Book of Jerry Falwell: Fundamentalist Language and Politics.* Princeton, N.J.: Princeton University Press, 2000.

Jones, Bob, II. *Cornbread and Caviar.* Greenville, S.C. : Bob Jones University Press, 1985.

Liebman, Robert, and Robert Wuthnow. *The New Christian Right: Mobilization and Legitimation.* New York: Aldine de Gruyter, 1983.

Marsden, George. *Reforming Fundamentalism.* Grand Rapids, Mich.: William B. Erdman, 1987.

Peshkin, Alan. *God's Choice: The Total World of a Christian Fundamentalist School.* Chicago: University of Chicago Press, 1986.

Rice, John R. *The Home, Courtship, Marriage, and Children.* New York: Garland Publishing Company, 1988.

Riesbrodt, Martin. *Pious Passion: The Emergence of Modern Fundamentalism in the United States and Iran.* Berkeley: University of California Press, 1990.

Riley, William A. *The Finality of the Higher Criticism or the Theory of Evolution and False Theology.* New York: Garland Publishing Company, 1988.

Robertson, Pat, and Bob Slosser. *The Secret Kingdom.* Nashville: T. Nelson, 1982.

Shepard, William. "Fundamentalism: Christian and Islamic." *Religion* 17 (1987).

Wuthnow, Robert, and Matthew Lawson. "Religious Movements and Counter Movements in North America." In *New Religious Movements and Rapid Social Change,* edited by James Beckford. Paris: UNESCO, 1986.

## Islamic Fundamentalism

Ba-Yunus, Ilyas. "The Myth of Islamic Fundamentalism." *East-West Review* 1, no. 2 (Summer 1995).

Euben, Roxanne. *Enemy in the Mirror: Islamic Fundamentalism and the Limits of Modern Rationalism.* Princeton, N.J.: Princeton University Press, 1999.

Fischer, Michael. "Imam Khomeini: Four Levels of Understanding." In *Voices of Resurgent Islam,* edited by John Esposito. New York: Oxford University Press, 1983.

Gaffney, Patrick. *The Prophet's Pulpit: Islamic Preaching in Contemporary Egypt.* Berkeley: University of California Press, 1994.

Gibb, H. A. R., and J. H. Kramers, eds. *Shorter Encyclopedia of Islam.* Ithaca, N.Y.: Cornell University Press, 1953.

Hegland, Mary. "Two Images of Husain: Accommodation and Revolution in an Iranian Village." In *Religion and Politics in Iran,* edited by Nikki Keddie. New Haven, Conn.: Yale University Press, 1983.

Ismail, Salwa. "Confronting the Other: Identity, Culture, Politics and Conservative Islamism in Egypt," *International Journal of Middle East Studies* 30, no. 2 (May 1998).

Kepel, Gilles. *Muslim Extremism in Egypt: The Prophet and the Pharaoh.* Berkeley: University of California Press, 1984.

———. *Allah in the West: Islamic Movements in America and Europe.* Stanford, Calif.: Stanford University Press, 1997.

Khomeini, Sayeed Ruhollah. *Islamic Revolution: Writings and Declarations of Imam Khomeini.* Translated and annotated by Hamid Algar. Berkeley: Mizan Press, 1981.

Lawrence, Bruce. *Shattering the Myth: Islam Beyond Violence.* Princeton, N.J.: Princeton University Press, 1998.

Mawdudi, Sayyid Abul A'la. *Let Us Be Muslims.* Edited by Khurram Murad. London: The Islamic Foundation, 1985.

Middle East Research and Information Project (MERIP). "Islam and the State," no. 153 (July–August 1988).

Mir-Hosseini, Ziba. *Islam and Gender: The Religious Debate in Contemporary Iran.* Princeton, N.J.: Princeton University Press, 1999.

Moussalli, Ahmad S. *Historical Dictionary of Islamic Fundamentalist Movements in the Arab World, Iran, and Turkey.* Lanham, Md.: Scarecrow Press, 1999.

Munson, Henry. *The House of Si Abd Allah: The Oral History of a Moroccan Family.* New Haven, Conn.: Yale University Press, 1984.

Mutahhari, Murtaza. *Islamic Hijab: Modest Dress.* Chicago: Kazi Publications, 1988.

Niblock, Tim, and Rodney Wilson, eds. *Islamic Economics.* New York: Edward Elgar, 1999.

Olivier, Roy. *The Failure of Political Islam.* Cambridge, Mass.: Harvard University Press, 1994.

Qutb, Sayed. *Milestones.* Cedar Rapids, Iowa: Unity Publishing Company, n.d.

Rahman, Fazlur. "Islamic Modernism: Its Scope, Method and Alternatives." *International Journal of Middle East Studies* 1, no. 4 (October 1970).

Shepard, William. *Sayyid Qutb and Islamic Activism.* New York: E. J. Brill, 1996.
Starrett, Gregory. *Education, Politics and Religious Transformation in Egypt.* Berkeley: University of California Press, 1998.
Zeghal, Malika. "Religion and Politics in Egypt: The Ulema of Al-Azhar, Radical Islam and the State (1952–54)." *International Journal of Middle East Studies* 31, no. 3 (August 1999).

## Jewish Fundamentalism

Aran, Gideon. "Jewish Zionist Fundamentalism: The Bloc of the Faithful in Israel (*Gush Emunim*)." In *Fundamentalisms Observed*, edited by Martin Marty and Scott Appleby. Chicago: University of Chicago Press, 1993.
Cromer, Gerald. "Withdrawal and Conquest: Two Aspects of the *Haredi* Response to Modernity." In *Jewish Fundamentalism in Comparative Perspective: Religion, Ideology, and the Crisis of Modernity*, edited by Laurence Silberstein. New York: New York University Press, 1993.
Falah, Ghazi. "Recent Jewish Colonization in Hebron." In *The Impact of Gush Emunim: Politics and Settlement in the West Bank*, edited by David Newman. London: Croom Helm, 1985.
Friedman, Robert I. *Zealots for Zion: Inside Israel's West Bank Settlement Movement.* New York: Random House, 1992.
Friedman, Menachem. "The State of Israel as a Theological Dilemma." In *The Israeli State and Society: Boundaries and Frontiers*, edited by Baruch Kimmerling. Albany, N.Y.: State University of New York Press, 1989.
———. "The Market Model and Religious Radicalism." In *Jewish Fundamentalism in Comparative Perspective: Religion, Ideology, and the Crisis of Modernity*, edited by Laurence Silberstein. New York: New York University Press, 1993.
Heilman, Samuel. *Defenders of the Faith: Inside Ultra-Orthodox Jewry.* New York: Schocken Books, 1992.
———. "Quiescent and Active Fundamentalisms: The Jewish Cases." In *Accounting for Fundamentalisms*, edited by Martin Marty and Scott Appleby. Chicago: University of Chicago Press, 1994.
Kahane, Rabbi Meir. *Never Again: A Program for Jewish Survival.* New York: Pyramid Books, 1972.
Lustick, Ian. *For the Land and the Lord: Jewish Fundamentalism in Israel.* New York: Council on Foreign Relations, 1988.

Perlmutter, Amos. *The Life and Times of Menachem Begin.* New York: Doubleday, 1987.

Silberstein, Laurence. "Religion, Ideology, Modernity: Theoretical Issues in a Study of Jewish Fundamentalism," In *Jewish Fundamentalism in Comparative Perspective: Religion, Ideology, and the Crisis of Modernity,* edited by Laurence Silberstein. New York: New York University Press, 1993.

Sivan, Emmanuel, and Menachem Friedman. *Religious Radicalism and Politics in the Middle East.* Albany, N.Y.: State University of New York Press, 1990.

Sprinzak, Ehud. *The Ascendance of Israel's Radical Right.* New York: Oxford, 1991.

———. *Brother against Brother: Violence and Extremism in Israeli Politics from Altalena to the Rabin Assassination.* New York: The Free Press, 1999.

Tal, Uriel. "Foundations of a Political Messianic Trend in Israel." In *Essential Papers on Messianic Movements and Personalities in Jewish History,* edited by Marc Saperstein. New York: New York University Press, 1992.

Weisburd, David, and Vered Vinitzky. "Vigilantism as Rational Social Control: The Case of *Gush Emunim* Settlers." In *Religion and Politics: Political Anthropology,* Volume 3, edited by Myron Aronoff. New Brunswick, N.J.: Transaction Books, 1993.

OPEC (Organization of Petroleum
Exporting Countries), 19, 33n38,
134, 148n2

Pakistan, 87; banking in, 157
Palestine/Palestinians, 25, 98, 99,
147, 155, 156
patron-client ties, 9, 31, 34n56
Peshkin, Alan, 61
phenomenal perspective, viii
pilgrimage (Muslim), 96, 136; "little"
('umra), 141
pluralization of private beliefs, 20, 154
political party (*hizb*), 59, 60, 61
Pope John Paul II, 42
power relations, shift in, 11, 160
prayer: Friday congregational, 91; and
Shi'ah Muslims of Iran, 96
preacher(s): and activism, 90;
contaminated, 74; college in
Jordan, 136; as culture broker,
31n14; Protestant, 155; sermon,
150n18; traveling, 135; of village,
6, 7, 60, 61
Presbyterians, 23
proof-texts (biblical), 39, 155; and
ethics, 63
Protestant churches: *See*
churches
Protestant fundamentalists, 39
Protestantism, progressive/patriotic,
17, 18, 154
protest movements: religious, 15;
urban, 23. *See also* movements

Quran, x, 6, 8, 18, 21, 37, 39, 43, 44,
59, 79, 81, 85, 101, 139; chanting
of, 101; reading of, 143; and

stipulated punishments, 46;
teaching of, 135, 136; and
television, 127; verses of, 40, 100,
144, 147, 158
Qutb, Sayyid, 22, 45

Reagan, President, 42, 107, 120, 121
rebbe, 57, 87; from Brooklyn, 85
relativization of public values, 20, 154
religion: and anthropology, viii;
bureaucratization of, 135–36; civil,
12; and learning, 135, 148n4; of
the people, 74, 90–92; popular, vii;
of the state, 74, 90–93; and
violence, 104–5. *See also*
Juergensmeyer, Mark
religious change (resurgence), xi, 136;
and fundamentalists, 157. *See also*
religion, bureaucratization of
religious-minded people, 21
Riesebrodt, Martin, 22, 23
Roberts, Oral, 109, 110
Robertson, Pat, 22, 82, 105, 109,
130n19, 160, 161; and Christian
Broadcasting Network, 119
Roman Catholics, 24; in Latin
America, 26; in Italy, 28
Roosevelt, Theodore, 17
Rousseau, Jean Jacque, 14; Lloyd and
Susanne Rudolph, 8

salvation: quest for, 11, 105, 146, 153;
vocabulary of, 77
Satan, 21, 59, 104
Saudi Arabia, 22, 30n1, 90, 91, 124;
and concept of male protector,
126; and religious philanthropy,
136

scripturalism, xii, 2, 155; and the
mosque, 158
secularism, 28, 87
secularization, 20. *See also* secularism.
See also secular society
secular nationalism, 14, 15
secular society, 85, 86, 92, 117
Shi'ah (Shiite) Muslims, 22, 42, 97,
113n42; of Iran, 51n17, 94; ethos
of, 95; and prayer and intercession,
96; and theology, 95
South Africa, 49. 64, 65, 70, 155
Spiro, Melford, xiiin2
Stoll, David, 26, 27
Straton, Reverend John, 38, 41
Sunni Muslims, 95
Swaggart, Jimmy, 110

Talmud, 47, 85
televangelism, 108–11, 119
television, 42, 94; and evangelists,
105; in Egypt, 124–25; in Lebanon
(Hezbollah), 127. See also
televangelism
Terry, Randall, 89
theology, x, 15, 113n35; and
metaphors, 68; Shi'ah, 95
time, ecological and ritual, 9
tithing, 58
Torah, 25, 85, 162n5
total institution, 40; and
confrontational fundamentalists,
111
totalism, 2, 156; and orthopraxy, 158;
and total teaching, 78; as world
view, 97

traditioning, 2, 155; defined, 156; and
sex roles, 63; in the U.S.A., 61
Traditions of the Prophet, 328, 43, 85,
146; defined, 151n29; and
fundamentalist view of, 138, 144;
teaching of, 135
transnational migration, 10, 13,
148n1; in Jordan, 134
transnational, religion, 2; and Falun
Gong, 153, 162n4; and Saudi
Arabia, 136
Tunisia, 91
Turkey, 87, 156
Tylor, Edward, xiiin2

'ulema (Muslim scholars), vii, 74; and
Shah of Iran, 113n42
United States, xi, 12, 13, 15, 157;
fundamentalists movements in, 91;
televangelism in, 108–11

veiling, 1, 30n1, 45, 87, 97
Virgin Mary. *See* Mary

westoxification, 114n47
Whyte, William H., 117
Wilson, Woodrow, 17
world view: organic, 11, 154; of
fundamentalism, 16, 128, 148, 155,
160

yeshiva, 57, 87; and Dr. Baruch
Goldstein, 102
Yiddish, 56, 57

Zionism/Zionists, 19, 56, 69n8

Richard T. Antoun is professor of anthropology at the State University of New York at Binghamton. A Fulbright Scholar and past president of the Middle East Studies Association, he has taught at Indiana University, Manchester University, England, and as visiting professor at the American University of Beirut and the University of Chicago. On the basis of extensive field research in Jordan and Iran over the last forty years, Antoun has written three books: *Arab Village: A Social Structural Study of a Transjordanian Peasant Community* (1972); *Low-Key Politics: Local-Level Leadership and Change in the Middle East* (1979); and *Muslim Preacher in the Modern World: A Jordanian Case Study in Comparative Perspective* (1989). He has also co-edited three interdisciplinary volumes. His interests include comparative religion and symbolism, local-level politics, peasant and post-peasant societies, and transnational migration. He has just completed a book manuscript entitled "Transnational Migration in the Post-Modern World," describing and analyzing the implications of transnational migration for higher education and work from Jordan to Europe, Asia, the Arabian Peninsula, and North America.